Threading Beads

A Millennium Anthology

Stories of Betrayal and Discovery

Published by

women's ink

publishing

Edited by

Geraldine Horan & Michelle Wright

Published by

614 Fulham Road
London SW6 5RP
Phone: +44 020 7371 9549
e-mail: womens_ink@liv4now.com

Typesetting, layout and
Book Cover Design by
Russell Blake

ISBN: 0 9539691 0 X

Printed in the UK by
Prontaprint (Fulham)
December 2000

Acknowledgements

We gratefully acknowledge the support of Hammersmith and Fulham Community Liaison who awarded Women's Ink an initial millennium grant which enabled us to apply for further funding.

This book would not have been possible without the generous support and funds received in the form of the Millennium Festival **Awards For All** Grant from the National Lottery Board.

There are many who have given their time and encouragement. These include (in alphabetical order) Anthology Committee (Geraldine Horan, Michelle Wright, Jeanne Mullane, Val Creegan, Lucy Edwardes and Caroline Walker), Paul Bickerton, Bernie Donovan, Mrs. C. Granville, Rosemarie Hayden, Nomad Bookshop, Mary O'Leary, Joe Ramalho, John Reed, Eckhard Thiemann (Arts Team of Hammersmith and Fulham Council).

Finally, our sincerest thanks to all members of Women's Ink and also our families and friends, who have supported us not only as writers, but also in bringing this exciting project to fruition.

Introduction

Women's Ink, formerly known as Wednesday Women originated from a creative writing course run by Hammersmith and Fulham Learning and Leisure, in 1991. Our tutor was Josie Pearse and the course was held on Wednesday afternoon at Fulham Cross Centre.

Our group grew and membership increased dramatically over the years culminating in our first Anthology, produced after two years of intensive commitment and dedication in 1994. We now felt confident enough to run the group as a workshop and called ourselves Wednesday Women. We continued to meet on Wednesdays but, due to popular demand for evening meetings, changed the venue to Nomad Bookshop, 781 Fulham Road, who graciously allowed us the use of their downstairs premises.

Other Anthologies have followed, resulting in our current Millennium Anthology, Threading Beads sponsored by Hammersmith & Fulham Council and The Lottery Awards For All Millennium Festival Grant. This is our most ambitious project to date which endorses our policies of encouraging and supporting women from all cultural, educational and social backgrounds to practice their craft and to get published.

Bernie Donovan
(Founder Member)

CONTENTS

Foreword

Threading Beads, our Millennium Anthology is based on the themes of Betrayal and Discovery. The pieces range from short stories, extracts of novels in progress, poems, prose and a play. A vibrant, eclectic collection of original works weaves a rich textural literary tapestry.

The themes are deliberately broad in spectrum to encompass and emphasize the diversity and complexity within our group, allowing our writers freedom to express their individuality.

The works are presented by contrasting our authors and alternating between the light and dark, comedic through to touchingly tragic, a kaleidoscope of emotions, literary forms and styles.

We hope you are stimulated and enjoy our Anthology and are encouraged to start writing or go back to your craft and support other women writers in their quest to be published.

Geraldine Horan
(Anthology Chair)

Kate
Lord Brown

Kate was born in Warwickshire, and grew up in Devon. After reading Philosophy at Durham University and Art History at the Courtauld Institute of Art, she worked for a visual and performing arts festival. Since 1995 she has been Associate Director of a Chelsea based international art consultancy, and a Fellow of the Royal Society of Arts since 1999. She has just written her first novel 'Love and Loss', and plans to write full time. She is married, and lived in London until recently - she's now travelling the world.

COMPANY

The sign above the door said 'Mes Amis', the hard edge of the neon softened by the rain that ran over its twisting tubes like quick tongues round candy canes. 'Mes Amis'. What a misnomer,' I thought as I saw the notoriously aggressive landlord throw another drunk out onto the pavement. I watched as the man lay there, talking to his own reflection in the window. A car drove past sending a shower of water from the gutter over him. He didn't notice and went right on talking to himself, the streetlights washing away on the glassy pavement around him.

I forced my attention back to the cast meeting. Margot was sitting at the head of the table, waving her arms as she spoke. I sat at the other end, the actors in our company between us. Margot insisted on the usual symmetry, as if we were still married, rather than just director and producer. 'Did she choose this place deliberately?' I thought. I swirled the ice around in the base of my heavy tumbler, the condensation cool against my fingertips. 'She knew I'd hate it.' It was times like this I could really do with a proper drink. I glanced at the window again, and then at my watch. 'She's late,' I thought. 'Boris has probably taken the long route from the airport. I know I would have done if I'd had the chance.' My eyes flickered over Margot's face. I can hardly bear to look at her these days. She's just a constant reminder of everything that's gone. Behind her, I saw the reflection of a man, and it took me a moment to realise it was my own image floating wretchedly in the gloom. The lighting in the bar accentuated the heavy lines on my tanned face. I ran my hand through my hair as I looked away. I felt tired, and old. I needed a haircut. 'Boris must be around the same age as Eva,' I thought. It bothered me, the thought of her with him. 'Eva can handle him though,' I told myself. 'She can take care of herself if he ever … But he's a good-looking guy. Any woman would be flattered. Who am I kidding?' I thought.

Distantly, I heard Margot still chattering on and on about the production. 'Why did she insist on a meeting tonight of all nights,' I thought. 'She knew Eva was flying back into London.' I glanced over at Margot. As she smiled at one of the cast, her eyes bulged like a panting Pekinese. She had cerise lipstick smeared across her teeth, I saw with distaste. God how that stuff used to cling to the glasses at home. The last time I kissed Eva good bye, she had just eaten a slice of a Cox's apple, and she still smelt sweet and clear. I love apples too. I beckoned to the waitress,
'Same again,' I said, placing the empty glass on her tray. My voice sounded alien to me, as if someone else had spoken.
'Sure thing,' she said. 'Get you anything else?' she asked, giving me the eye. Maybe she had recognised me. It happens a lot.
'Pascal, what do you think about Act II?' Margot asked loudly, her voice cutting through my appreciation of the waitress like an unseen gull screeching in fog. She glared at the waitress as she spoke.

The girl was pretty in a bland way. Not beautiful, like Eva, though she was around the same age. I shook my head and smiled as she shrugged her shoulders, then looked at Margot. 'Act II? What do I think of Act II,' I mused. I stood and put my hands in my pockets. Through the hole in the left one my fingertips brushed my thigh. It felt illicit somehow, to be touching myself so intimately, but I kept my hand there all the same. I loomed over the table like a mountain backlit by the sun. 'Perhaps you should ask your leading man,' I said, leaning on the table with the other hand. The shadow I cast across them lengthened as I leaned closer to Margot. She sensed my mood immediately and backed down.

'When he turns up of course I will,' she said quietly.

'Boris can't be much longer,' one of the company giggled, and Margot glared at her furiously.

I sat down again when the waitress brought my drink over. Just then some guy came in at the door, shaking the rain from his hair. I caught Margot looking up at exactly the same time as me, and we both looked away disappointed. She shuffled her papers, and began to discuss the casting again.

I sipped my drink. 'What I wouldn't give for a shot of bourbon,' I thought. 'Just the one. But Eva hates it when I drink.' Margot carried on discussing the casting. 'Maybe I'll take a part this time,' I said suddenly, and the whole table turned to look at me. I hadn't meant to say it, I had just been thinking it to myself. If it hadn't been for the shock on their faces I would have questioned if I'd said it out loud. You know how sometimes you say something and then can't remember five minutes later if you'd actually said it or if you were just wondering about it, but you don't want to run the risk of repeating yourself and looking an idiot? That happens a lot to me lately.

'But you haven't acted for years, not since Eva left in fact,' Margot said with a clipped tone to her voice.

'Well maybe it's about time I did,' I said, swaggering slightly.

'But who would produce the show then?' she said, her eyes narrowing.

'I would, as usual,' I said, squaring up to her. 'I didn't say I wanted the lead did I? Just a small part, that's all I want in anything, now that Eva's gone.' She looked away.

'I don't know how Boris would feel about being on the same stage as you,' she muttered, shuffling the pages of the script. 'Even in a minor role, you would completely overshadow any attention paid to him.'

'Poor Boris,' I said sarcastically.

'What is it with you? What have you got against him?' she said, scattering her pages on the table. Everyone seemed to be receding until it was just the two of us there. It seemed like she was very close to me. I felt too hot, the smoke and the noise made my head swim. 'It's Eva, isn't it?' Margot laughed finally, folding her arms. 'You're jealous about Eva.'
'Don't be ridiculous,' I said too quickly. 'Jealous?' I thought, 'Of course I'm jealous. Eva. That was always my favourite name. Now I hardly ever get the chance to say it aloud, although I think about her all the time. I want to jump up on the table and yell her name until she comes running to me again. Right now Boris is no doubt chattering away as he drives her here, Eva this and Eva that. It's come to this. Now I'm jealous even of her name.'

'Eva!' Margot said suddenly, and I turned to see their figures in the doorway. Eva was handing Boris the jacket that he'd given her to shelter from the rain. 'How chivalrous,' I thought dryly, and had to fight the urge to run to her and take her in my arms. There was a time when she would have run to me.
'Hi everyone!' she called brightly. She had grown thinner I thought. 'Everyone' leapt up to kiss them both and I hung back as Margot fussed around them. I saw Eva glance at me once or twice, uncomfortably, the way I look at Margot sometimes now. 'How did it come to this?' I thought. 'How did all those years of loving her come down to this, more awkward than strangers who at least give one another the benefit of the doubt.'
'I think we're about done,' I heard Margot say.
'The ballet starts at 8.00,' Eva said to Margot. 'We'd better hurry or we'll be late.' I saw Boris' face fall. So did Eva. She turned her body into him and spoke quietly. As she did so, I saw his stupid handsome face light up like a Christmas tree. I made a mental note to play poker with him sometime. It would give me the greatest pleasure to take him to the cleaners. So Boris was

going to see her later. What about me? As they turned to go, Margot took pity on me. She spoke quickly to Eva. I was too disappointed to come forward. Eva walked towards me. She looked so beautiful, she took my breath away. There were so many questions I wanted to ask her: was she happy? Did she like living in the south? Did she still like cinnamon toast for breakfast? She looked at me with those sad eyes of hers, and smiled, nervously.

'Hi Dad,' she said, and kissed me gently on the cheek.

'Eva,' I said, and squeezed her hand. It fell like a wounded animal to her side.

'I've got to dash,' she said, her voice disjointed. 'Mum booked these tickets months ago. Perhaps I'll see you over the weekend.'

'When are you leaving?'

'Sunday night.' Her eyes flickered to her mother and the door.

'So soon?'

'I have to work!' she laughed, backing away. 'I've got to go.' She turned and I watched them walk off. The breath caught in my throat as I waited for her to turn to me once more, to smile and wave, but I found myself, one hand still raised, no longer waving, staring at the door as it closed softly behind them. The rain still slicked down the panes. Was that it? Was that what I had been looking forward to for weeks? My baby and her mother. The women I love more than any other in the world, walking away again. I am alone, again. How did it happen? How did it come to this? All for one minor indiscretion, some waitress whose name I can't even remember. Yes I betrayed them, but at least it was quick and sharp, and they moved on. Their betrayal is more treacherous. They wield the enduring disappointment that has covered my life like a cape of pale fog, deadening my senses, killing every pleasure in my life. 'Forgive me,' I said. 'I'm sorry,' I said. Even then they turned and walked away leaving my sorrow to drift on and on. Perhaps we betrayed each other, in our ways. I was weak, but they were strong. Lost in the fog of my own life, lost in blind misery, lost without them, I sensed that Boris had been hovering at my side for some time, and pulled my attention back to the surface, and the noise of the bar flooded in.

'Buy you a drink?' he asked cautiously. I nodded dumbly, and joined him at the bar. His question was a relief. I thought for one dreadful moment that he was going to ask my permission to marry Eva. It seemed appropriate somehow; two disappointed men together while two bright, happy women went off into the night. I envy them their easy relationship. I miss the company of my women. I miss the colour they brought to my life. There are too many bars and too many waitresses like this one. 'Bourbon, on the rocks.' They are only attractive when you have a home to go to. I miss my life, my home, my wife, but more than that I miss my child, my baby bird, my Eva. Eva, Eva, Eva, like a sigh. Where did you go?

MISS LA LA AT THE CIRQUE FERNANDO

'Welcome to the greatest show on earth,' the ringmaster bellowed as he cracked his whip. The Easter crowds thronging the Champs Elysées cheered as confetti fell about their heads. Somewhere a trumpet sounded. Friends and lovers, and families in their holiday best packed the pavements, waiting for the parade to begin. The boulevards were strung with silver lights like fireflies in a lilac sky rich with the scent of roasting nuts, fried onions, sugar canes and hot chocolate. From the shadow of the Arc de Triomphe, gleaming horses with crimson ribbons in their tails reared and pranced, leading the way for jugglers and acrobats. Gymnasts cartwheeled down the road as floats with caged wild cats rolled past. Clowns waved to the crowds and handed out balloons and printed sheets. An expectant hush fell on the streets, the trumpet voluntary grew and fireworks burst gold and blue against the night. In silhouette she stood astride the backs of two pacing white horses, her arms raised to the sky. The cheers rang out: 'Bravo Miss LaLa,' they cried. She threw back her saffron silk cape, the horses thundered down the street. The Cirque Fernando was in town.

My grandmother, LaLa to her friends, was a remarkable woman. She stood over six feet tall, and had hair as rich as the last tongues of a sunset quenched in a fire-eating sea. Her mother and father (a trapeze artist and a lion-tamer respectively), were not unusually large, and her stature was proudly attributed to the bloodline of her great uncle, a strongman venerated throughout Europe for his performance at the Winter Palace in St Petersburg in 1793. Ever since he dragged the Tsar's coach from one end of Nevsky Prospect to the other with the Tsar and his family on board, we have been circus aristocracy. His legendary status was ensured when he was killed tragically young, hit in a freak accident by a human cannonball.

She smelt of the south my grandmother, of warm air and rosemary, of open roads and dusty tracks in fields of lavender. Those who knew her intimately said that when she let her glorious red hair down, the gilded tips brushed her ankles. It was as white as cirrus clouds by the time I was old enough to remember her, and she was a little bowed, but in her youth she had been courted by every strongman, lion-tamer and sword-swallower in Europe. Many men loved her, but none had won her hand, and at the age of 29 the star of the Cirque Fernando resolutely remained Miss LaLa.

'It is hard to be a strong woman,' my great grandmother had told her on her death bed. 'It is better to be alone than be with a man who tries to make you weak.' With that, she smiled and closed her eyes. Her devoted husband died within days, leaving Miss LaLa queen of her own caravan, and mistress of a pride of lions. Tales of her skill and beauty spread throughout the land. On the night of the parade in Paris, in an inn by the coast, a would be suitor known as Claude heard Miss LaLa spoken of in reverent tones by two grown men who wept into their ale with comradeship and longing as they told anyone who would listen how they had tried and failed to win her heart. Claude was a bare knuckle boxer. He was the undefeated champion of the finest circus rings on mainland Europe. He had heard of the legendary Miss LaLa, and over time he formed the opinion that she would be his ultimate challenge. Claude's caravan walls were decorated with the stuffed heads of wild animals he had captured on his hunting trips between fights. He set out to win her heart with the same combination of brute determination and hot blooded lust he had felt when pursuing wilder quarry. With her name tattooed over his heart like a promise, he rode across France to Paris where he knew the Cirque Fernando performed for the Easter holidays.

Miss LaLa was sitting on the steps of her caravan combing her hair, singing a melancholy tune to the sunset as Claude rode into camp. She was thinking of nothing in particular, and she was as unaware as you usually are that her life was about to change. As Claude leapt off his stallion, the young groom Guy ran forward and soothed the trembling beast. Claude glared down and tossed him the reins.

'Is that Miss LaLa?' he grunted.

'Yes sir,' Guy said, lowering his head.

'This horse needs feeding. See to it.' Claude strode confidently across the field to where Miss LaLa stood, her chin raised.

'I offer you my heart!' he cried, and tore open his shirt as he reached the steps to her caravan. He fell to his knees reaching vainly towards her. He was a fine looking man, but he was not the first, and Miss LaLa restrained her natural passions with the same efficiency her satin corsets applied to her voluptuous figure on stage. She gathered up her skirts, affording him a tantalising glimpse of her trim ankles, and slammed the door behind her.

'By god,' Claude thought as he stared up at the red door of Miss LaLa's caravan, 'I've romanced the most beautiful acrobats and gymnasts that Schumann and Hagenbeck have to offer. I've loved women in Circus Knie, the pride of the ring at Elleboog and Boltini. But never, never, have I laid eyes on so fine a woman as that.'

Claude realised direct pursuit was hopeless. He soon established himself as a sideshow star at the Cirque Fernando, but did his best to avoid Miss LaLa at all costs, while cultivating his reputation with the other performers. One day as she tended her lions, Miss LaLa saw him walking with an acrobat on each arm. He saw her watching, and with one eye on her, left them there, bowing low. She hid as the girls walked past her enclosure, annoyed at how quickly her heart beat as one girl sighed:

'Claude is such a gentleman. Why, any woman in her right mind would be proud to have a man like that.'

'They say he's in love with Miss LaLa,' the other laughed.

'Poor man. Everyone knows no man will ever be good enough for our Miss LaLa.'

'Why all the men in France are too afraid to try!'

Miss LaLa sank to the floor and began to cry. A lion cub clambered onto her lap and licked her face. 'Perhaps it is better to be alone than tame,' she thought. 'But why does it have to hurt so much?'

As she stumbled from the enclosure, her eyes red rimmed and smarting, she bumped into Guy and sent him flying.

'I'm sorry,' she sobbed, 'I'm such a clumsy oaf.'

Guy blushed bright red, awed to be in the presence of the woman who filled his every dream and waking moment. She took his silence for agreement and began to cry again.

'No, no you're not,' he stammered, and placed a kind hand on her arm. He pulled a handkerchief from his pocket and handed it to her. As she blew her nose she noticed it smelt of warm hay.

'No wonder men are scared of me,' she sighed.

'Not scared,' he said, grasping his one chance. 'In awe perhaps.'

'I'm too strong for men,' she bit her lip anxiously.

'Never. You are a beautiful woman Miss LaLa. If only you knew ...' his heart thundered but he went on. 'If only you knew, there is a man who is very much in love with you. He thinks you never notice him, but he would do anything for you.'

Miss LaLa looked at Guy's imploring face, and past to where Claude was beating a navvie into a pulp against the side of the boxing ring, to the delighted cheers of the crowd. As the man fell, Claude looked up and caught her eye.

'You're right,' she said. 'Thank you Guy.' She bent down and kissed him gently on the cheek, and walked off towards her caravan, as Guy realised he had lost her to another, bigger man. That night at the inn as Guy drowned his sorrows, Claude stood centre stage as usual. The nightly lamentation of his love for Miss LaLa had begun to pall on even the most kind hearted of the circus folk, but he was too big and too cruel when drunk for any of them to shut him up.

'I don't know how to win her heart,' he sighed.

'I'll have you, anytime,' a gymnast cried, and the crowd laughed. 'Sunflowers,' Guy said, lurching to his feet and placing himself in front of Claude. His hazy focus settled somewhere near Claude's sternum.

'What?' Claude asked, and lifted him up. 'I can't hear you down there.'

'Sunflowers. Give her sunflowers,' Guy slurred.

'The boy likes flowers?' Claude mocked. Guy was well liked, but still they laughed at him, uneasily swayed by Claude. 'What are you? A poofter?'

Guy no longer cared, he nodded dumbly. 'Think what you will,' he thought as Claude pitched him back towards his table. 'If she wants you, what can I do? I only want her to be happy. Though I doubt she ever will, with you.'

Claude may have laughed, but all the same he took a huge bunch of sunflowers to Miss LaLa the next day. Guy was grooming her horse as she let Claude into her caravan. He leant his head against its firm flank, and something inside him died. The news soon spread of Claude and Miss LaLa's engagement. A traditional circus wedding was planned for the day after the last performance of the season.

'You are a brave man Claude,' one of the old gypsy trainers

teased him as they watched Miss LaLa practicing her act. 'She's a wild one for sure.'

'What do you mean?' asked Claude, unnerved to hear his own thoughts voiced aloud.

The old man lurched closer, and Claude could smell stale whisky on his breath. 'Why if she were a circus beast I'd pull her claws so she don't scratch, or clip her wings to make sure she don't stray at night.' He slapped him heartily on the back, and Claude's mind lumbered into action. He watched his magnificent fiancée perform the finale of her act, hoisted high above the safety trampoline which he well knew would not be there on the night. 'An 'accident' to keep her home,' he thought, chewing on a piece of grass. 'I couldn't. She trusts me too much.' He smiled at her and waved. She performed a double somersault in his honour.

The last show always had a magical atmosphere. The circus was sold out. Backstage, as Miss LaLa waited to go on, Guy stood by her side, with the horses. He knew this was the last time he would do this, and whenever she looked away, he gazed longingly up at her.

'I'll leave before daybreak,' he thought. 'I can't bear to see her marry that oaf. Perhaps when I hand her the horses tonight, I could just say 'Good Luck', and kiss her cheek gently ...' Lost in his adoration of her, he did not see Claude approaching.

'What are you staring at?' Claude bellowed, making them both jump. The horses reared, their hooves slicing into the earth. 'I've half killed men for looking at my women like that.' He cuffed Guy's cheek, catching him with the large ruby ring he wore when he wasn't fighting. Guy flinched as blood trickled down his face.

'Claude,' Miss LaLa raged. A crowd gathered around them. 'How dare you! Are you all right Guy?' she asked, gently dabbing at his cheek with a cream silk handkerchief she pulled from her magnificent cleavage. Guy's head swam with desire. He nodded dumbly. 'Get out of here Claude.' She squared up to him. 'Tomorrow I will be your wife. If you go around thumping every man who looks at me, what kind of life will we have? Trust me, as I trust you. I don't need anyone to fight for me,' she said as one of the trembling horses stamped on Claude's foot. He yelped, but Miss LaLa was not impressed. She kissed the horse's nose kindly. 'Just go Claude. Look how you've scared the horses.' As the crowd laughed, Claude limped away, his heart filled with a murderous desire for revenge.

'How dare she show me up,' he thought. 'I'll show her tomorrow, just you wait until we're alone ...' His eye fell on where the ropes for Miss LaLa's aerial display were tied. 'Why wait until then,' he muttered with a cruel sneer, as the trumpets sounded and Miss LaLa took to the ring. 'Perhaps if your wings were clipped, then you'd need me to fight for you.'

Miss LaLa stood astride her horses, racing round the ring as she welcomed the rapturous applause with open arms. Her favourite saffron satin corset girded her curvaceous figure like armour, as her strong feet gripped the horses' backs in sequined slippers. Her lilac satin cape fluttered behind her, flying up into the ochre dome of the circus tent as the ropes lifted her higher. She swung and flipped to 'oohs' and 'aahs', as at ease in the air as she was on the ground. Guy called to the horses, and they left the ring, joining him in the shadows. As Miss LaLa ascended to the rafters of the dome for the finale of her act, spinning from a rope clenched between her teeth, Guy inhaled the sweet scent of her handkerchief. Gazing up at the daring feat, he whispered, 'I love you,' and lowered his eyes. He looked for the last time around the circus ring at the open mouthed children caught up in her spell. Something on the other side of the tent caught his eye, a dark flash, the spotlight caught on Claude's ruby ring on the floor in the shadows.

'Claude,' Guy cried. It happened in a few seconds, but to Guy it was like a lifetime. He saw Claude's leering smile, the rope in his hands, and looked up to where Miss LaLa span high above the ground. By the time he looked back at Claude again, he saw the rope begin to loosen and snake. A cry went up in the crowd, there was no time to waste. Guy knew he could not reach the rope in time on foot. He leapt onto the horse. As they plunged into the ring, a mighty cheer went up. Guy balanced, and flung himself at the rope as they raced past. For a moment, he felt himself caught in mid air, but then, thank god, the weight of the rope in his hands. Though Guy kept on rising, he slowed her descent. In mid air their eyes locked, her face a picture of confusion. Ever the professional, Miss LaLa landed in the centre of the ring with a gracious curtsey to rapturous applause. The frenzy backstage was carefully hidden, and the crew let Guy down slowly. He was shaking uncontrollably as Miss LaLa took his hand for them to bow together, the audience convinced it was all part of the act.

'What happened?' she whispered to him as they left the ring.

'Claude,' he began to say, as the man himself raced to her side.

'My love,' he cried. 'Are you all right? What was this little fool doing? Trying to come between us - he could have killed you!'

'I'm fine thank you Claude,' she said carefully. 'Now what were you going to say Guy?' The crowd fell silent, as Guy cleared his throat.

'I'm sorry but Claude betrayed you, Miss LaLa,' he said. 'I saw him loosening your ropes.'

'Rubbish!' Claude bellowed. 'Prove it,' he said, bunching his fist at Guy's chin. Guy glanced down at this massive hand, twice the size of his own. He turned his calm eyes to Claude, then to Miss LaLa, and pointed to where the ropes were tied.

'Claude's ring,' he said. Claude stretched out his bare hands in alarm, but it was too late. Miss LaLa strode over and retrieved it herself.

'Get out of my sight!' she cried. Claude was booed from the tent.

We don't take kindly to betrayal by one of our own, and the tale of Claude and Miss LaLa spread throughout the land. He never worked in the circus again - no one could trust him, and in a profession like ours, trust is all. As for Miss LaLa, she may have been strong, but her big heart was broken. Sometimes though in our darkest hour, we see the light that shows us where our future lies. Guy didn't leave, and the next summer sunflowers bloomed again.

Often grandparents and grandchildren have an easier relationship than parents and their offspring. A warm and easy flow of love without demands and expectations grows. My mother prefers to call Miss LaLa an 'artiste' in much the same way she refers to treacherous Claude as an 'athlete'. I once heard my daughter, when asked about the Degas painting of her great-grandmother, refer to her in such mimsy terms. She shares my mother's delicacy and nimble fingers in embroidering the past. But we have our similarities. We are a family of tall red-headed women, and small dark men. We like it that way. What worked well for Miss LaLa has worked well for her daughters and granddaughters. We have enough strength to do the task of any man, so we have no need of musclemen. We like men who are kind, who we can laugh with and talk to, who we can clasp to our breast and dance with, men like my grandfather who bring us sunflowers when summer comes round.

Michelle Wright

Michelle was born and grew up in rural New Zealand. She attended university and trained as a primary school teacher. She taught in a small community before teaching English in Tokyo, Japan. To finance her travelling, she worked with children who have English as additional language in inner-city London schools. Michelle writes short stories for adults and picture books for children. She currently lives in Fulham with her husband and young daughter, but is shortly emigrating with her family to live in Melbourne, Australia.

STAGE FRIGHT

The shame crept into my face, leaking out and spreading like paste through my pores. Heat rolling off my nose in beads of sweat, and my hands wrenching my T-shirt tightly. I knew everyone was going to be looking at me, just me. It was all right performing as a group on the stage in front of our parents and families and friends of families, but it was not all right for them all to look at me. I will do it wrong. I know I will forget all the things I am meant to say. I know my voice will tremble and I will cry. In front of everyone.

My brother will tease me. He might not even wait till after the concert. He just might stand up right while I am introducing the group and say, 'Ha! Ha! You look stupid! You are stupid!' I feel stupid. I will tell mum that he is teasing me and she will tell him to stop. But he will only stop while she is listening. He will hiss 'stupid' through doors at me, push out his tongue behind mum's back and when my mum gets sick of hearing me complain about him, she will then yell at me. 'Oh! Don't let him get to you! That's all he wants!' He wants it and he has got it. Already.

No, I can't do it. I can't get up in front of that sea of people and introduce the Korokonui Every Girls Rally Christmas Concert. Mrs. Evans had us all assembled and Sophia hadn't turned up. Whenever we had practised, she had got up and in a very clear and strong voice had introduced all the songs perfectly. But, she hadn't turned up to the real thing. It was in the evening and we were all to come, and she hadn't. So now we have no introducer, and Mrs. Evans had scanned all our faces and had decided, 'Natalie, you can do it. You have a nice clear voice, and you know what to say. Just stand up and tell everyone welcome and what songs we are going to sing.'

And just like that I was the chosen one, and now she was sat before the piano and was banging out the good old favourite - 'Jesus loves me, this I know, because the bible tells me so.' It was a great one for settling the masses. It was telling the audience the concert was about to start, and it was going to be fun, but please be quiet.

Mrs. Evans often communicated through her keys.

She had changed the whole evening for me. There I was, proud in my blue serge wrap around skirt (I had heard my mum swear while making it on her old Singer machine, with a pattern borrowed from our neighbour). My netball T-shirt doubled up as the required white blouse and pinned proudly to my shoulder were my long blue straps of badges. I had earned them all by cooking, cleaning and making sand saucers. Odds were, that I was going to get a few more by the end of evening, and maybe even win a book for being the most cheerful girl at Rally. Though, not much chance of that now.

I scanned the door for Sophia, willing her to sail in and run up to her empty place, whisper sorry to everyone and asked if she had missed anything? But she didn't. Sophia with those lovely 'womanly hips' that could carry me like a baby, whose fingers pinched my cheeks lovingly until they were red and ached. Sophia, how could you do this to me? I thought you liked me, you always say I am cute and let me hang out with you, even though you would rather hang out with John, my oldest brother.

Just for a moment, I hated Sophia.

I watched the mums march one by one into the kitchen with their plate of food for the supper after, and I can see my mum talking in there with another mother. And it is starting! No Sophia! Mrs. Evans is busy banging on her keys, smiling madly at the audience and ignoring my dilemma completely. God, I hate her too.

The audience settles, Mrs. Evans changes tunes and all the girls come in on cue. I can't sing. I can't remember any of those words. All I can think is that I have about two minutes before the start of my shame. My downfall will begin. To be remembered forever as the girl who stammered and cried in front of *everyone*. The pressure was mounting, the song was in its final chorus, and I know what I have to do. I have to go. I just can't be there. I carefully crouch up and climb pass as inconspicuously as you can when getting over 10 sets of knees in the front row. I wind round the back of the girls standing and clump down the stage steps, through the back rooms that meet with the kitchen.

Mum thankfully, is still there, gassing with the other mother. Comparing the amount of eggs each of their sponges took. She looks at me with surprise, her eyebrows nearly touching her perm. I burst into tears to cement which side she will take and cry, 'don't make me do it!' She colours slightly in front of her sponge rival and hugs me to her legs. 'Well, I suppose they won't stop the show for you to go back now.' She has shown her support. She still loves me. Perhaps I will get that book after all.

I smile through my tears.

Dear Mrs. Evans,

I am writing to tell you how sorry I am for running out of the Every Girls Rally Christmas Concert and not introducing the songs and welcoming the parents like you asked me to do. I got very scared and very nervous and I thought I would make a mistake, and I hadn't practiced and I knew I wouldn't be as good as Sophia Jackson. She has a much clearer voice than me, and she doesn't get scared or go red. And she is the oldest in her family; she is much bigger than her brothers.

Thank you very much for giving me the bible study book for being a 'cheerful girl at Rally'. I certainly was after winning the book. I like the pictures. I am hoping that the camel can get through the eye of a needle.

Yours sincerely,
Natalie.

Dear Natalie,

I was very disappointed that you left in the middle of the concert and did not even try to make the introductions. The reason that I choose you is that you have a loud, strong clear voice. I should know, as I hear it each day in the classroom. In fact, I think you are the only student in the history of Korakonui School that has had chatterbox consistently mentioned on your school report.

After discussing the situation with your mother and Mr. Evans, we have decided not to punish you, but perhaps in class, (and in rally) you could be less vocal, then you might not be our first choice for getting someone to speak out loud.

Yours sincerely,
Mrs. Evans.

THE KUIA / THE GRANDMOTHER

The kuia sat on the top step of the veranda of her weatherboard house. The late summer sun frolicked on the leaves of the kahikatea and the pohutakawa tree, its red Christmas blossom beginning to gently shift and fall in the dry breeze. She looked down at her creased brown hands, knotted with age.

'Aue', she sighs to herself.

Muffled squeals of delight rose from the two children, playing on the grassy bank in front of the house. Rawiri, the elder of the two cousins, had tied Hone's skateboard onto the back of his bike. Hone with unsteady seesaw arms was attempting to grass ski down the slope, towed by his cousin's Raleigh chopper. The kuia could not remember exactly whose offspring these children, her mokopuna, belonged to, however she could vividly recall those days when she was as young as they. In her minds' eye at that moment, it was she playing on the same grassy knoll, and it was her grandmother sitting on this same doorstep, drinking in the unfailing blessings of Ra, the Sun God. Longevity had created a jumbled notion of time, and now she was it's matriarch.

'Aue', she repeated.

In a brief moment of clarity, something in the kuia beckoned the shrill funeral wail, the karanga that would guide her spirit from this world into the next. It was true, there existed within her a deep longing, as far reaching as the roots of the kauri tree, to be once again with the loved people of her iwi, who had travelled this passage before her.

She knew her time was near, and she was not frightened.

Catching snippets of Maori pitched from the boys reminded her of her first days at the Pakeha School. The hot sticky feeling of shame, when Mrs. Cook had slapped and chastised her for speaking her native tongue. Now all her mokapuna were educated at Kohanga Reo, the full immersion Maori language school, speaking their pictorial and lush language with pride. She had been told that now all the kids of New Zealand learnt Maori, even at the pakeha schools.

Aue, things have changed in the cycle of time.

Shifting her ungainly body, the kuia raised slightly the black cotton of her skirt to let Ra's tingling fingers massage her aching knee joints. Too much pork and puha for this wahine. Not like her skinny granddaughters! Sucked into the waif-like fashion of the pakeha. They, who do not appreciate the wealth associated with fatness. The kuia recalled the tourist photos with skinny wahine dressed in the traditional flax skirt, offset by the rich bubbling mud-pools and geysers of Rotorua. The deep tattoo outlining her lips and chin, her moko, quivered in the slack skin as she chuckled at the pakeha's image of a 'beautiful maori woman'.

A black fantail, with it's twittering song landed on the wooden rail beside her. Looking at her, his black beady eyes spoke of her children and her children's children. They had returned to the marae, they did not know or feel shame in things Maori. They had returned to learn the ways of the old, the carving of the bone and the highly prized greenstone, the plaiting of the flax and the making of the tukutuku panel that adorned the walls inside the large meetinghouse. These mokopuna, playing so innocently before her, knew their whakapapa, their genealogy.

And an inner calm, a repose, flooded into her large body.

'Aue.' She said no louder than the last, outgoing breath.

The kuia heard the ghost of death sing gently to her.

'E tama, i whanake	'O child, winterborn
i te ata o pipiri	Rise up and join
Piki hau ake, e tama	your forbears'
Ki tou tini i te rangi.'	in heaven.'

'Rawiri! Tai ho!' puffed Hone. The bailing twine had wound around and lodged itself tightly in the wheels of his skateboard. 'I's nearly gunna crap off then,' exclaimed Rawiri. Straddling his bike, he leant forward and with delicate precision, hoiked a fat globule of spit and hit his cousin fair square on his knee.
'Piss off! Ya Shitface!' yelled Hone.
'Try 'n make me, sissy teko bum!' retorted Rawiri pulling out his invisible mere, the flat, fighting club, from the waistband of his jeans. Making the cry of an ancestral warrior, he rolled back his eyes and leapt down to beat up his younger cousin. The fight exhausted itself to a plague of giggles.

The contagious laughter extended up to the figure of their grandmother, perched like a black crone on the front steps of the house. They were both aware that their grandmother's poor hearing and eyesight allowed them to swear, spit and fight each other in reckless abandon. Something that would surely earn them a clip around the ear, should their Uncles or Aunties be about.

'Looks like she's gunna croak it,' howled Rawiri with tears of laughter pooling in his eyes. Hone puckered his lips and imitated the sounds of the frogs that lived in the pond at the bottom of the gully.

Another luxury of childhood naughtiness, to disrespect elders, but only when they're not about to hear you, eh?

'She's too buggered to help us,' said Hone motioning toward the black silhouette of their grandmother.
'Maybe she can bring down a knife to chop through this,' replied Rawiri inspecting the tangle of bike chain and twine with his grimy fingers.
'I'll give you a bloody good hiding if I catch you fool'n with that knife again!' shouted Hone, mimicking their Uncle Joe, who would give them a 'bloody good hiding' for most things fun to play with.
'But, we won't get into trouble if she brings it down,' said Hone.
'Yeah, and I can't be arsed going up to get it', agreed Rawiri.

The conspiracy passed in a look between them.

'Eh, Nana!'
'E Kui, haere mai!'
'E pou!'
'E Nnnnaaaannnnnaaaaaaa!'

Their shouts cut through the stillness of time and space and were lifted and stretched out to one long mournful wail.

A karanga to their dead grandmother.

Doreen Isherwood

Doreen is a Chartered Physiotherapist specialising in Women's Health at Queen Mary's Hospital, Roehampton. She has written for medical journals on the value of massage for mothers and babies and the use of Reflexology in women's health. Originally from Lancashire, she has lived many years in Fulham and has three children and two grandchildren.

LEARNING FOR LIFE

The woman sat on the front step, last year's brown felt slippers punched out of shape by painful bunions. The other two women leaned against the wall, looking down on her. Mrs Bibby and Mrs Thomas (nobody ever called them by their first names, not even their husbands) wore identical floral aprons which encompassed their substantial girths.

Mrs Bibby was short and toothless - she did have a set of false teeth which on the important occasions, when she manoeuvred them into her reluctant mouth, made her look like a startled monkey. Her bishop's apron of a belly could be constrained by a whalebone corset, but only with the breathless assistance of Mr Bibby as he tightened the laces over her spreading flesh. Her thinning hair was tortured into metal curlers, her pink scalp showing raw between the irregular rows. Now and then she scratched with a none too clean fingernail as rogue strands of hair pulled too tightly against the shining curler. Myopic blue eyes bulged behind the thick lenses of her pink framed glasses - she didn't trust that Irish doctor who'd given her tablets for her thyroid, so she'd thrown them on the back of the fire.

Heavy gold earrings dragged her lobes down a full inch, the holes gaping from repeated attempts to reopen them with a darning needle. They'd closed up several times over the years while the earrings languished in Manny's pawnshop waiting to be released. Wrinkled brown woollen stockings concertinaed over her faded tartan slippers, small holes roughly cut out to accommodate her throbbing corns.

Her neighbour, Mrs Thomas, was a good head taller, her usually untidy mop of dark hair tucked into a white turban - her badge of office at the Home and Colonial Store where she reigned supreme on the bacon counter. Her left cheek was covered by a port wine stain, which she halfheartedly concealed with panstick make-up. She favoured bright red lipstick that clung tenaciously to her Player's cigarette, eventually dragging away paper and a few strands of tobacco that she spat out at regular intervals. Varicose veins hung uselessly behind her left knee and her swollen feet bore testimony to the long hours spent behind the counter. The Irish doctor wanted her to have the veins removed, but what did he know? She'd probably come round from the operation to find her leg missing.

The two women sighed in unison and adjusted their breasts with their forearms as they looked down on Mrs Holcroft. All three had been at school together, found jobs locally and married boys they'd known forever. That was the way of it. The boys joined the ranks of workers at the engineering factory and spent their free time at the works' social club, rolling home to fish suppers before the nightly ritual of locking up, seeing that the fireguard was in place and winding up the clock on the mantelpiece. There was no need for an alarm. The factory obligingly roused the whole neighbourhood at 6-30 each morning with its keening siren.

The three women had bred small families - the priest held no sway over this enclave. Mrs Bibby had two sons who were now apprenticed at the works and earning enough money for their keep and a couple of pints of beer each night. They eyed the local talent but that's as far as it went.

Mrs Thomas had a remarkably pretty daughter who had just left school and was about to start work as a junior at the hairdresser's in the high street. Her son rode a delivery bike for the Home and Colonial thanks to his mother putting a word in.

He spent his spare time fishing with his father, enjoying the peace away from the women's chatter.

Mrs Holcroft had only one child, a daughter, who was clever - too clever by half. What could be done with a girl who won prizes at the grammar school and wanted to go to the university? It was unheard of.

'She should be out at work now, bringing some money in'. Mrs Bibby was the first to put in her two penny's worth.

'Aye, put your foot down and don't be so daft with her. Who does she think she is, turning her nose up at us all? Nobody likes her, you know.' Mrs Thomas was always a bit of a stirrer.

The girl in question was up in her bedroom at the back of the terraced house, preparing an essay on evolution. That anyone should be in their bedroom in the early evening without being ill was most peculiar.

'She'll get brain fever, working like that,' said Mrs Thomas for good measure.

The two women began to move away. The men would be disgorged from the factory soon and there'd be hell to pay if the tea wasn't on the table. Mr Thomas ate a lot of bacon without complaint and Mr Bibby would eat anything as long as it was covered in gravy and piled up with chips.

Mrs Holcroft roused herself, eased her bunions into a more comfortable space in her slippers and stood up. Seemingly unmoved by the comments of her neighbours she nonetheless lifted her chin and gave them the benefit of a particularly straight look before they turned towards each other and raised expressive eyebrows.

She made her way down the narrow hallway to the small

kitchen, which smelled faintly of gas. Sitting on a plate on the draining board were three mackerel, their eyes blank and dull. She considered them - they didn't look very fresh but they were cheap and fish was reckoned to be good for the brain, wasn't it?

Mr Holcroft trod wearily down the hallway and passed her on his way to the outside lavatory. They had a bathroom upstairs now but he preferred to go down to the end of the small backyard where he could have a smoke and read the racing page in peace. The pungent smell of frying fish drifted up to the bedroom. The girl wrinkled her nose in disgust. She hated mackerel and felt a familiar spasm of guilt as she was well aware that life would be so much easier for everyone if she took a job locally and brought in some much needed money.
'It's on the table, love'. Her mother's muffled voice emerged from the kitchen.
She stretched and put the top back carefully on her pen before running lightly down the dark stairs to join her parents at the table.

The overhead light bathed the trio as they tackled the fish and reached for the stack of bread and butter - no margarine in this house, thank you very much.

Mr Holcroft was a small wiry man with thinning brown hair recently cut into the regulation short back and sides. Despite giving his hands a good scrub in the kitchen sink, the ingrained oil still lined his fingernails and blended with the nicotine stains on the first two fingers of his left hand.
As he carefully arranged the treacherous fish bones round the rim of his plate, he glanced across at his wife, caught her eye and winked.

My, but she'd been a good looking girl - heavy dark hair

swinging across her cheek as he partnered her at the local hop. She was a great dancer and didn't try to lead as most of the other girls did.

Now her hair was streaked with grey but she refused to have it dyed and swore by rinsing it in vinegar to bring out the shine. She dressed neatly and didn't make a show of herself. He was very pleased about that. Nobody could accuse his wife of looking like mutton dressed as lamb. Her skin was clear and unlined except for two deep creases between her eyebrows, which were more noticeable when she'd been at the receiving end of unwanted advice from her two particular friends. A dab of Pond's cream worked wonders usually.

She was a good mother. Pity they'd only had the one child but she'd been so poorly after the birth of their daughter that he'd decided that enough was enough. Never mind what his mates said, he couldn't go through that again.

He watched his daughter dutifully dissecting the oily fish. Her dark hair was drawn into a ponytail, the ends broken where she chewed them during spells of intense concentration.
The small face of a Timex watch peeped out below the sleeve of her white school blouse. He had given it to her when she passed the scholarship to the Grammar School. He adored his daughter even though he found it hard to understand why she'd turned out so differently from the other kids in the street. It wasn't from his side of the family, that's for sure. Perhaps it was something to do with being an only child. There weren't many of them in this neck of the woods. Mind you, his wife had been a bit sharp as a nipper but she'd outgrown that early on.

All in all, he was content with his lot. He was the man of the family, the breadwinner - a good feeling despite the ribbing he suffered from his mates at the social club.

The girl raised her eyes from the skeleton on her plate and exchanged a rueful smile with her mother who was mopping up rogue flakes of fish with the remaining piece of bread.

'Not keen on mackerel, are you, love? Never mind, it's cod and chips tomorrow. That'll do your brain just as much good and at least we'll all enjoy it'.

Mrs Holcroft loved her daughter with an intensity that surprised her. Nobody she knew spoke about these things and indeed, most families were daggers drawn with the occasional truce. Even now as her daughter travelled down an intellectual path she felt inadequate to follow, there was an unshakeable bond which held them together. She colluded with her in her quest to push back the boundaries and escape from the limited future that confronted her.

As a girl, Mrs Holcroft, Mary Forbes as she was then, had suppressed her keen intellect in order to appease her family and friends. Her membership of the local library was regarded as a waste of time and praise for her work by the teacher was sure to lead to ribald comments after school. Mary confined herself to reading her father's newspaper before it was cut into squares and attached to a nail in the lavatory. No sense in wasting a good bit of paper.

She had nurtured her daughter's budding intellect, withstanding the mockery of the neighbours and accepting the unquestioning support of her husband. It was easier to champion her daughter than stick up for herself.

The sight of books on the shelves in the back bedroom gave her immense pleasure, as did the virgin sheets of white paper waiting for the first stroke of the pen. All this had been denied her until her daughter had braved the scorn of childhood friends and had thrown herself into an orgy of learning.

Was it too late for her to jog her brain into gear? Had she let herself fall too deeply into inertia? Could she write anything of greater significance than a short message in a Christmas card? With her daughter's help she might.

The girl was humming as she gathered up the plates and carried them to the kitchen sink.

'I'll just wash these up while Dad makes us a pot of tea. You sit down now and have a rest.'

The armchair did look inviting. It seemed a long time since the two of them had snuggled into the cushions with the first reading books, enjoying the adventures of Rupert Bear and singing nursery rhymes. 'Mary, Mary Quite Contrary' was always a favourite.

'You're dozing off there. Let me pour you a nice cup of tea now it's brewed. I know, I know. You only like your china cup and saucer. Anybody would think you're the Queen Mother. I'm going out to the darts match when I've got changed. They're putting sausage rolls and meat and potato pies on after so don't bother to leave me any supper.'

He whistled tunelessly as he climbed the stairs. A man at ease with his world.

The girl emerged from the kitchen shaking out the red and white tea towel before hanging it near the fire to dry. She sniffed her hands, caught a distinct fishy smell and instinctively recoiled before laughing at her mother's 'don't you dare' expression.

She knelt by the chair, feeling her mother's hand gently stroking the top of her head.

'You know that book we were looking at the other night - you know, the one with the list of classes you can take at the Tech?

Well, how about trying for the one on local history? You could probably tell them a thing or two, couldn't you?'

'Oh, I don't think Dad would like that. Me going out to the Tech. He'd think I'd gone barmy. And what would my friends say? They tormented me enough when we were young and they're still going on about you. I can't do it.'

'You've wasted yourself all these years, Mam. You know that. Don't let that pair rule your life. Now you talk to Dad about it if you want to. I'm sure he won't mind when he gets used to the idea.'

'I'll ask your Dad tomorrow.'

'Why not tonight before he goes to the club?'

'Oh no. I'll have to think about it first.'

'O.K., but I'm not going to give up so you'd better get your thinking cap on quick.'

With that, the girl kissed her mother's hot cheek and stood up.

'I've just got a couple of things to tidy upstairs. Won't be long.'

Left to herself in the armchair, Mrs Holcroft sighed. Yes, she would love to try the class, although she was a bit worried that the other people would know a lot more than she did. Was she up to it? She'd be the target of her neighbours' jibes and no doubt her husband would have something to say. Wives round here didn't go to classes and he might think that his womenfolk were getting above themselves. 'Peas above sticks' was one of his favourite expressions.

'I'm off. See you later.'

With that, Mr Holcroft banged the front door and fell in step with one of the darts team who was passing by.

The heat from the fire was making her bunions throb which at least took her mind off the prospect of asking her husband's permission to go to the Tech.

She stood up, easing her back and feet before repeatedly running her fingers through her hair as the conflict raged within.

The re-opening of her long-suppressed urge for learning was uncomfortable and often unwelcome as she resisted her daughter's eager encouragement to take those first steps. There was a sharp rap on the front door and a voice called through the letterbox.

'We're popping up to the Bingo for an hour. Are you coming?' Mrs Hibby and Mrs Thomas enjoyed the odd night out when their husbands had gone to the Club. They had to be back in time to make their suppers though.

'No thanks, not tonight. See you tomorrow.'

She couldn't face a session at the Bingo Hall among the regular crowd of women with eyes riveted to the sheets of numbers and fingers gripping their lucky marking pens. Then later there was the endless talk of how they'd only needed one number to win. No, not tonight.

'Hey, you sound like a herd of elephants coming down those stairs.'

'Sorry, Mam.'

A quick grin and the girl was back by the fire.

'I could murder some chips. Shall we nip round to the shop?'

'Get the coats then while I put some shoes on. A bit of fresh air will clear the cobwebs.'

After putting the guard round the fire the two of them set off arm in arm to walk the couple of hundred yards to the chip shop which was run by Betty Murphy or Sweaty Betty as the kids called her.

'Chips and mushy peas twice. We'll have them open.'

'You don't usually come in on a Tuesday night. Having a change, are you?'

Betty didn't wait for a reply.

'Still working hard at school, are you?' she asked as she scooped the hot chips onto greaseproof paper.

'Yes. I've got my exams soon,' the girl replied, eyeing the bright green mushy peas being ladled over the waiting chips. Betty gave her a pitying smile as she scattered salt and vinegar from a great height.

'Well don't strain your eyes with all that reading,' she advised, giving her steamed up glasses a quick rub with the corner of her grease-spotted apron.

Betty took their money and they called good night before walking slowly back home, savouring every mouthful of the satisfying supper.

'Mmmm. I'll miss this when I go off to college.'

Mrs Holcroft experienced a gut wrenching pang which had nothing to do with the chips and peas.

She must make her mind up about what to do with herself when her daughter had left. If she began now, with her strong support, she could handle the inevitable lapses in courage in the face of opposition from the others.

They reached home, ready for a good cup of tea after the greasy food.

In the kitchen, vaguely aware of the background smell of gas and mackerel, mother and daughter moved through the familiar routine of making the tea and setting out their favourite cups and saucers.

'Well, Mam?'

'I'll try.'

'Good'

They turned towards each other, blue eyes level, a mixture of love, fear, understanding and excitement shared between them. It was no longer young Mary Forbes on her own. It was Mary Holcroft and Daughter. The one she'd named Hope.

YESTERDAY'S FRIEND

Today he is my enemy
Yesterday my friend.
What's the sense in all of this?
When will it ever end?

Today we madly hate and curse
Yesterday we loved.
What's the sense in all of this?
When will it ever end?

Today we starve across the street
Yesterday we shared.
What's the sense in all of this?
When will it ever end?

Today we shoot to maim and kill
Yesterday we played.
What's the sense in all of this?
When will it ever end?

Today he died my enemy
Yesterday my friend.
What's the sense in all of this?
When will it ever end?

STOP THE ROT

Aching joints
Easing

Woolly mind
Clearing

Flushing face
Cooling

Wrinkling skin
Smoothing

Thinning bones
Building

Leaking bladder
Holding

Waning libido
Rousing

Oh, the wonders Of HRT
So they say.

Jay Merrill

Jay has had several short stories published in anthologies and magazines, and she had a short play performed at the Lost Theatre's One Act Festival in Fulham, in 1999.

Jay also hosts live poetry events, currently at the Raj Tearooms in Highgate where she also reads some of her short fiction. In addition, Jay judges the short story competition SOLITAIRE, for the St John on Bethnal Green Summer Arts Festival.

Jay is now working on the first draft of her novel and hopes to complete in the new year.

THE FREEDOM TREE
A ten-minute one-act play for Stage

THE CURTAIN RISES. THE STRANGER STANDS IN THE CENTRE OF THE STAGE. AT THE REAR IS A LARGE SCREEN WITH THE IMAGE OF A BOY WRIGGLING HIS FEET AS THOUGH IN PAIN. HE STARES FORWARD AND MAKES NO SOUND.

THE STRANGER

You were wailing in the street this morning and your little anxious feet were grinding against the insides of your coarse canvas shoes.
But your eyes were dry. You would not let the tears be seen.

CLOSE UP OF BOY'S FACE ON THE SCREEN. AS THE STRANGER SPEAKS THE BOY COVERS HIS FACE WITH HIS HANDS.

THE STRANGER

There are many things, which you should know which you do not know. You should know how to do your sums, like the others. You should know how to spell and to write clearly enough for the letters to be readable. You are afraid about what will happen to you because you cannot do these things.

THE SCREEN IS NOW EMPTY AND CONTINUES SO

DURING THE FOLLOWING SPEECH. THERE IS THE FAINT SOUND OF DISTANT SIGHS.

THE STRANGER

You shiver as you come up to the stone porch and the ominous doorway with the flight of stairs just inside. Even though the time is past and you are no longer vulnerable.

DURING THE FOLLOWING SPEECH THE EMPTY SCREEN GETS BRIGHTER VERY GRADUALLY, UNTIL IT IS RADIANT.

THE STRANGER

The school is lighter now. You used to think of it as blind. There was a lot of yellow in the grey walls but not of sunshine. Now, there are many colours. You see the plane tree from a new glossy window at the end of the corridor. The sight warms you as always.

THE SCREEN IS NOW FULL OF RADIANT LIGHT.

THE STRANGER

Get up of a Sunday morning. Sunshine if you're lucky, no wind. Step out from all the dull chaos of Jupiter Buildings. Step out. Quite soon you are feeling free. Sunday morning in summer. No school.

Vauxhall Bridge Road. Feeling free. Kick the
dust up with your heels. See it rising, up and up.
Francis Street, Willow Place. All dusty-
sunshine. If you're lucky. My ghost is a small
boy. He has things to tell. Things like these.
Most of all he will want to talk about the tree that
made thoughts of freedom possible. The tree
was unbelievable and the tree was a friend.

THE SCREEN FADES TO EMPTY. THE STRANGER
STEPS FORWARD ON THE STAGE TO BE AS CLOSE TO
THE AUDIENCE AS POSSIBLE.

THE STRANGER

There is a special way in which your voice
comes to me. It passes through buildings and
across distance as though they did not exist. In
my mind but not of my mind, with the weight of
brick, the lightness of air. The kind of
knowledge I have of it is intuitive. There's a
shine to it, and an echo.

THE STRANGER STARTS TO WALK ABOUT THE STAGE,
LOOKING AT THIS AND THAT, AS THOUGH ON A
SUMMER'S WALK.

THE STRANGER

It is summer. I am passing the tall gates of
the school playground. I stop and look through.
The plane tree, very green. A circular seat runs
round the trunk.

THE BOY (VOICE OVER)

That never used to be there.
We just used to stand under the branches and
keep out of the rain. I had just started school and
the only thing I wasn't frightened of was the
tree, but when the weather got cold the leaves
fell off and left it all bare. I was so sorry.

DIM LIGHTING. FACE OF BOY ON THE SCREEN EYES
PUCKERED WITH PAIN.

THE STRANGER

Chill November. You shiver. A small boy, going
to school perhaps. It's just past 8.30 in the
morning. You are afraid of being late like
yesterday. The headmaster caned your hand and
tears squeezed out of the corners of your eyes
even though you tried to stop them.

PUCKERED FACE OF BOY ON SCREEN AS A SEPIA
PHOTOGRAPHIC STILL.

THE BOY (VOICE OVER)

At break-time it is raining. Puddles are forming
in the uneven dips of the playground.

THE STRANGER

As you stand beneath the tree, sheltering, you

see a yellow leaf swirling slowly then coming
suddenly to the ground beaten down by rain.

THE BOY (VOICE OVER)

Did that leaf come from the tree?

PAUSE
ON THE SCREEN IS A DIM OLD FASHIONED KITCHEN
WITH A WOODEN FOOD CABINET.

THE STRANGER

The kitchen in Jupiter Buildings is small and dim
with a tall wooden cabinet where food is kept.
You climb in the bottom cupboard to hide and
the cabinet topples and then crashes against the
opposite wall. Milk, jam, sugar and salt all spilt.

SEE THE CABINET FALL FORWARD ACCOMPANIED
WITH A CACOPHONY OF HARSH VIOLIN SOUNDS.

THE BOY (VOICE OVER)

It is shocking the way it lurches forward, and
that huge shadow….. Mingled foods. Powder
turning moist, becoming slop.

SCREEN TURNS TO COMPLETE BLACK. A DISTANT
RUSTLING SOUND, AS OF A TREE.

THE STRANGER

The voice of the dead, remote yet right here. An echo, a shadow which stops when I stop, waits while I listen.

A LARGE YELLOW LEAF FLOATS DOWN ONTO THE STAGE.

THE BOY (VOICE OVER)

Where did that leaf come from? Did it come from the tree? Is the tree dying then?

THE STRANGER

I hear you having this question in your mind.

ON THE SCREEN THE BOY IS HOLDING A VIOLIN AND A BOW AS THOUGH HE IS PLAYING.

THE STRANGER

I hear violin music, a sequence of notes. Beautiful. I see you standing with the violin in your hand in the front room at Jupiter Buildings. A small boy, sparse, and uncertain eyed. Oh what powerful beauty.

ON THE SCREEN THE BOY IS PLACING THE VIOLIN IN ITS CASE. HE STARTS TO UNBUTTON HIS SHIRT.

THE STRANGER

You are afraid to go on, in case….. in case you lose

the beauty. You lay down the bow. But also, how terrible to make it happen. All that beauty pouring out of you, surrounding you and weighing you down. That would really make you cry. Such force. Everyone would see your elemental tears.

ON THE SCREEN THE BOY IS PULLING ON A WHITE RUNNING SHIRT WITH A LARGE NUMBER ON IT, AS THOUGH FOR A RACE.

THE STRANGER

Going to run in the canvas shoes when all the others have spiked boots. 'Not fair,' I hear you say. The sharpness of the cinder track which cuts into your feet. But you will not stop, you did not.

FADE THE SCREEN TO EMPTY.

THE BOY (VOICE OVER)

How did it happen that all the others knew what to wear and I did not? I was the odd one, the stupid one. And I could've beaten the lot of 'em.

THE STRANGER

With the right running shoes you could have. You feel a fool, you wish you were dead.
You wish you were invisible.

THE SCREEN GRADUALLY LIGHTENS TO RADIANT AS PREVIOUSLY. OVER THIS IS A VERY FAINT HUBBUB OF DISTANT VOICES.

THE STRANGER

So many terrors. So many things you do not know.
It makes you wail.
But, it's Sunday. No school. You are walking to Arthur Street to visit your cousins. A breeze, a bit of sun. You speak secretly to the tree from inside your heart. You run. Vauxhall Bridge Road, Rochester Row. Your cousins will be at the house combing their hair. You will catch sight of their eyes in the mirror. You will smile. There will be warmth and commotion, there will be talk. The horrors of school will fade. I have this very clear awareness that you want to tell me you sometimes feel alright about things.

THE SCREEN NOW BECOMES EMPTY. FOR ONE MOMENT THE STAGE GOES DARK AND WHEN THE LIGHTS COME BACK THE BOY IS STANDING AT THE CENTRE OF THE STAGE.

THE BOY

A magical thing has happened. The leaves have come back.

THE SCREEN CONTINUES EMPTY.

THE STRANGER (VOICE OVER)

You stand at the base of the trunk in spring
sunshine. You are small, the trunk is vast. You
think, 'The life in the tree was hidden. There was
no green but now it is full of leaf. The tree is
glorious. It knows how to conceal its life, how
to be invisible. And when the right moment
comes it can flourish.'

ON THE SCREEN IS NOW THE IMAGE OF THE
STRANGER.

THE STRANGER (VOICE OVER)

The tree sways gently in the wind.

THE BOY WALKS OVER TO WHERE THE LEAF IS LYING
ON THE STAGE.
HE BENDS DOWN AND PICKS IT UP.

THE BOY

One day, when I am dead, I will come here and
live inside this tree. I will sway to and fro with
the leafy branches. Sometimes I will be invisible
and sometimes I will shine.

CONTINUE WITH IMAGE OF THE STRANGER ON THE
SCREEN UNTIL THE END OF THE DIALOGUE.

THE BOY

Sometimes I will share my memories and my music with strangers and tell them about the special freedom I have found.

FADE TO BLACK.

I'M A GIRL. I'M NOT SILLY.

I'm four. Sometimes I'm a soldier. I march with John through the cornfield. I can keep up with him. I like poking a stiff grass blade between my teeth and whistling and swinging my arms and defying the enemy who hide behind the hedge when they see us coming.

John has friends who come from school. They are all fat boys with watches. I am thin, but I'm good at being a bird. I pretend-peck at crumbs on the lawn and I flap. Maybe they'll need a bird in one of the games. Yesterday I ate an ant which I'd caught on the end of a stick. I told them it was sweet. They said, 'Eer!'

When his friends come round John is not so friendly to me. If I've got Goldie Doll with me or Knitted Rabbit I'll talk to my toy so he'll see I'm busy and don't care.

- Georgie, Georgie, what you doing?
- I'm playing a game, so there.
- Georgie….. Georgie.
- What now?

That's the Fat Boys calling across the fence, John as well, and me calling back to them.

- Can you growl?
- Yes, I can!
- Show us, then.
I do a growl. They laugh.

- That's not a proper growl. Can you be a tiger with claws?
I throw my arms forward. - Pretend my claws shoot out.

- Pretend we've got wings and can fly.
They all run out of their garden and stand on the pavement. I run out of mine and stand with them.
- I've got wings now, - I say.
I hop and flap. I like being a bird. - Watch me.

All the boys are laughing. I laugh. They start to run back to John's garden. I run.
- We've got wings and we can fly after the Penguin. - John, calling as he runs.
- Bad luck Penguin.
They are running to the gate at the side of John's house. I run behind them. They run in the gate. The slowest Fat Boy gets there before me. They pull him in. The gate slams. I want to get in. I must. I can't. I lean against the gate. It's too heavy. It won't open. I kick it.
- Bad bird - they yell.
- Bad Bird!
- I want to play!
- Bad luck Penguin.
Another time:
- What shall we be?
- We'll be animals.
- I know, the animals all have to go together behind the curtain.
- I'm being a lion, - I say.
They start to run.
- The animals have to hide properly. - Voices jolting as they go.
I run but I am slower than the slowest animal.
- There's not room for the last animal. Lionie is not going in. Horse is going in, and Rhino's going in, and the water pistol can go in. - (They've got a water pistol).
- Goodbye Lionie.
The gate slams. They aim the water pistol and spray me from the top of the gate. Their feet scrabble against the bars. It's a

mad rush to reach the top. Heads pop up. Water sprays in my face.
- Cry baby.
- I'm not.
I shout. I kick the gate.
- Girls are silly.

- D'ya wanna play at ghosts?
- Look, we're ghosts.
- Can I be a ghost?
- Yes. You can be a ghost.
They're letting me. I'm happy. I make a long whistling noise and run with my arms stretched out as they do. But I am slower than the slowest fat-boy-ghost. The gate slams. I am pressed against it. They lean hard then they all jump back. The gate swings open. They roar. I rush to get in. It slams. It opens. I rush again. It closes slowly.

Running as fast as I can. If only I can be faster and get inside the gate. I want to get into the garden. I want to play. If only I could be faster. Just a bit. I'm nearly fast enough, nearly as fast as the slowest Fat Boy. Faster. Run faster! My legs race harder than ever before, but still I am just behind. The gate slams. It isn't fair.
Next time I'll make it.

Hot, fast, feet hard on the ground. Falling. Getting up again. Not crying, going. Into John's garden. Down the path. Feet running in front of me. Feet of the boys. Past the pinks, past the marigolds. Next, the roses. Blobs of colour on the way to the gate. Pink, gold, red. Nearly. Nearly got there.
The gate slams.
- Baby, Baby!

Blurred gold and pink, sky blue blurred in my head, patches of green; the lawn. Brick red corner of the house. Looming gate, dark as anything. Tall gate, angry gate.

I hate that gate. Feeling hot and prickly. Blobs of colour. Swooping. Fast. Pink faces turn and laugh. Teeth. Tongues sticking out.

- MerMer - Tongues.

Backs of heads, heels. Gate opens. A scramble. My hands reach out. Gate slams. My hands hit against the grainy wood.

- Mer Mer M Mer Mer.

But I'm four now and I shan't cry!

- I'm a girl. I'm not silly.   - I shout.

Rude crackly farting noises from behind the gate.

Jeanne Mullane

Jeanne was born in Scotland of Irish and Scottish parents. She has lived in Fulham for most of her life. After studying History and Education at Digby Stuart College, she taught in a local school. Then tutored adults learning English as a foreign language.

She writes short stories and is interested in writing plays and is hoping to complete a novel.

FORTY ACRES AND A MULE

Daniel woke with a start of fear. For a few seconds his terror at the consequences of being late overwhelmed him, but only temporarily. As he reached full consciousness, he realised that the unimaginable had come about. There was no one left to administer the punishment he dreaded, the scars on his back would not be lacerated again with the fierce sting of a bullwhip. He sat and listened. Silence. The strangest manifestation of these strange days, was the silence from the rows of meagre cabins adjacent to his mean shack. The silence, from outside, with no bells ringing to summon the workers to the fields, which were also silent and empty; no mules or creaking carts dragging their loads interminably to and fro. There were no sounds of whips cracking through the air or the sickening noise they made when they reached their target of human flesh. And most mercifully of all, no screams or wails from those unfortunate enough to transgress the rules. There was no rough cursing from the overseers, urging idlers on. There was no sound of hooves or gunshot from the slave patrols, riding round the plantation on the lookout for runaways.

Daniel remembered the day before when he had gone into the empty plantation house. He had walked through the lavish, silent rooms, all the laughter, talk, music and dancing had vanished and he felt like a ghost. It was only when he stood outside and looked up at the grand house, now like a vast porticoed mausoleum, that he really believed that the family had gone. That his master had gone. As he stood there transfixed, Eli, one of the house slaves, came up behind him.
'They're sure gone, they got word that General Sherman's men are 20 miles away, they just upped and left, in one big hurry.'
Daniel shook his head in wonder.

'They've gone, Daniel, you're free.'

Daniel smiled at him, and started walking back to slave row, into the middle of a great celebration. He was greeted with gleeful shouts from all sides.

'Jubilee is here, we're free!'

'It's the time of glory, Daniel, Freedom!'

He was grabbed and pulled into a group of dancers. He danced and laughed for joy, the joy of being free, free at last.

As the inhabitants of slave row slumbered after their revels, Daniel rose and went outside. It was not quite dawn, but the sky was lit up with a strange orange glow. With a shiver of fear, he realised that the burnished sky was the reflection of some great, destructive fire not many miles away. It seemed that General Sherman's men must be very close now.

The next day the union army arrived, followed by hordes of ragged refugees who, abandoned by their masters, with no food or shelter sought haven with their liberators.

The soldiers looted the house, and set fire to it. The heady smell of magnolia, which used to drench the summer air, was replaced by the acrid smell of burning. What was once Eden for the cosseted planter's family, was now reduced to a desolate wilderness. When the army set off again a few days later, Daniel decided to follow the itinerant throng, in the hope of finding his father and sister who had been sold some years before. That cruel transaction had caused his mother to sicken and die, inconsolable at the loss of her beloved daughter.

General Sherman led his army and its band of followers towards the sea. He commandeered acres of abandoned lands, which were divided into smallholdings, on which the nomadic camp followers were settled. This was the culmination of a dream for all those who had spent their life in bondage. Their simple request for 'forty acres and a mule' to live their life independently, was now granted. Daniel never located his father and sister, but in spite of this, he was content as he worked his small piece of land. He believed the golden dawn of prophecy had arrived and he had reached the Promised Land, but an assassin's bullet brought about great changes, and from Washington it was decreed that all confiscated land should be restored to its original owners. The soldiers came and Daniel and many others were evicted. And so he found himself again working on a plantation, no longer a slave, but still breaking his back, on a piece of land he did not own, for a share of the crop that he could barely subsist on. It meant his dreams of freedom were betrayed and his heart broken by promises unfulfilled.

Daniel watched the wild geese wistfully as they glided above him, so numerous they almost concealed the autumn sky, in their yearly migration south for the winter. He painfully contrasted his own position with theirs, and envied them their freedom. One night he heard the sound of hooves, he looked out. They rode past, their white robes flowing behind them, looking like the ghostly host they purported to be, soldiers risen from the dead to avenge the confederacy. Daniel frozen with fear held his breath until the sound of the horses faded into the distance. Haunted by the knowledge that yet another man could be hanging from a tree while his home was being burnt to the ground.

Whilst enduring impoverishment, and frequent terror, only the thought of taking part in the forthcoming election, in the hope of redressing the iniquity of his life, kept a spark of optimism alive in Daniel. On the day of the election Daniel set off cheerfully, but as he approached the voting booth, a man stood in his way. His face contorted, and red with rage.

'I'm telling you boy,' he said contemptuously.

'There's a coffin waiting for you, if you vote wrong.'

Daniel had to summon up every atom of courage he possessed

to walk past this threatening figure, and with shaking hand, he cast his vote. That night they came to his makeshift shack. They dragged him outside. There were three of them, menacing in their disguise, only their eyes visible. Their voices muffled, they did not appear to be human, seeming more like diabolic manifestations, from some dark, dreadful other world.

'We'll teach you to be so uppity boy,' one of them snarled. 'You'll pay for ignoring advice.'

They whipped him brutally, with such ferocity he almost lost consciousness. After they left, he lay on the ground, the blood oozing from the deep gashes on his back, saturating his shirt and he wept. Daniel decided then that he would have to leave the south.

As he crossed the Mason Dixon line, Daniel did not look back at the land where his ancestors had lived and toiled for two hundred years. Instead, he looked up at the Northern Star, which had guided so many runaway slaves to freedom. As it glittered in the midnight sky he fervently hoped it was an omen for him, of a better future...And meanwhile on the battle fields, the moonlight shone on the delicate spring flowers that had started to grow above the last resting places of fallen soldiers.

URBAN DECAY

The laughter and shouts of the four boys echoed across the empty expanses of mountain and bog land. As they ran joyfully, hither and thither through the furze, in search of the small brown wren traditionally hunted on the day following Christmas.

'There's one!' shouted the smallest of the four, a gentle eager boy of ten, small for his age with beautiful soft brown eyes. He was at the same time, vulnerable and exuberant. The wind and excitement of the chase had brought a rosy glow to his cheeks. He was enjoying himself so much with his brother Tim and their two friends, Pat-Joe and Con, as they roamed the familiar country close to their homes, he felt he could burst with happiness.

This irrepressible quartet lived each carefree moment to the full no shadows of future sorrow, clouded their present joy. As they approached their prey the delicate, frightened bird flew heavenwards and escaped. The pale blue sky was now fading to dusk, and the mild soft air was tinged with an almost imperceptible chill so they decided to abandon their hunt and return home.

It was good to come back into the warmth and comfort of a blazing, aromatic fire. They sat round its welcoming glow, and listened to their father's tales, of ancient myths and heroic stories of more recent events. While their mother prepared a meal for them, the smell of newly baked bread drifted deliciously round the room and on the large wooden dresser what was left of the Christmas cake sat temptingly on a china plate, its fruity aroma redolent of Christmas luxury. Surrounded by so much comfort and warmth, the young boy felt the happiness expand within him, like a bubble. He looked out of the window, at the silver dusted sky, and believed he could see the special Christmas star shining on him and blessing him. He could see the Christmas candles, twinkling with welcome from the windows of all the houses in the distance, sparkling like diamonds in the winter darkness. That night he drifted off to sleep contented and secure. The memory of that Christmas would come back to him with painful clarity on Christmas days spent in London because he could not afford the fare home.

It was ten years after that Christmas that he left home, like so many others before him to find work. He would never forget that journey, the misery of travelling down the mountain road, to the station in the pouring rain, or the tears of the people at the stations he passed on the way. These scenes of farewell, glanced at through the train window wrenched his heart, as he thought of his recent goodbye to his mother. The journey by boat, during a storm, had been uncomfortable and the wretchedness of seasickness made him very glad to reach land although he then had another long train journey. At last he arrived in London, which he found overwhelming and bewildering. He was very glad he had an address to go to, his old friend Pat-Joe would help him settle in.

At first it was strange to live in such a built-up, noisy place, so different from the space and silence of home. But there was plenty of work, and lots of cheap accommodation, and he gradually got used to it. He adapted to the work on many different building sites, in all weathers, and the often shabby, cold lodgings. In the end, he almost got to like it. He did sometimes think of home, with a sense of longing. But after his mother died, to his great sorrow, shortly after his father, he had no inclination to return.

The years passed, and he was fortunate enough to find some really good lodgings. The landlady and landlord were from his own place, at home. The house was clean and warm and the other tenants were his friends. It wasn't a bad life. He had his routine of work and many enjoyable evenings in the pub. He also loved to read and listen to the radio in his cosy room. Another ten years passed in this reasonably contented way. But his serenity was shattered when the owners of the house died within six months of each other. The nephew, who inherited the house, wished to sell it, and as a great profit could be made from selling it empty, all the tenants were given notice. So he found himself homeless and also without work. He had reached pensionable age and there was a recession in the building trade, nobody would employ him.

For the first time in his life he had to deal with the Social Services. He was apprehensive as he waited to be seen in the busy council office. He felt shabby, unsophisticated, and ill at ease. He was not used to dealing with bureaucracy. The woman who interviewed him appeared hostile and unsympathetic. She had a very officious manner, and he felt as if he was being interrogated. She peered at him through her glasses, asking him to repeat everything, evidently his accent was difficult to understand. She kept mispronouncing his name, in spite of his gentle corrections. He felt like a criminal as he explained that he never had a pension because of the lump system of payment that operated on building sites. He was not married and now had to leave his present accommodation. After having to fill in various forms and going to different departments, he left with relief. As he travelled home on the bus he felt humiliated and vulnerable. He supposed he had been foolish and he should have made more provisions for this time in his life, but you don't imagine yourself getting old.

He was eventually sorted out by the authorities and given a small flat at the bottom of a large tower block, in a big anonymous council estate, at the other end of the borough from where he had always lived, far away from all his friends. He realised he should feel grateful, the flat was newly decorated, with central heating, and a nice kitchen and bathroom. But the estate depressed him. It was a harsh, drab collection of concrete and glass, which drained the life and soul of all those who lived there. His heart sank every time he returned to his flat. The block where he lived reminded him of a prison, it was so stark, grey and cold. The gangs of youths that hung around frightened him. They laughed and jeered, and called him names whenever he walked passed them and once a lout threw a bottle at him, which just missed his head. He rarely saw the other tenants.

At first he used to get the bus down to his old haunts, though lately many of his friends had died, and the area was changing. The old community he had known was being dispersed. There were no rooms to let anymore, the prices of the houses were so high only the very rich could afford to live there now. Even the pub he used to frequent was under new management and had been refurbished to attract a younger, more fashionable clientele.

It was about this time that his arthritis began to get worse. His limbs were very stiff and the bronchitis, he was bothered with every winter, made him so breathless he could barely walk to the bus stop. He went out less and less, no one came to visit him, it was too far for his old friends to travel and they were ageing too. One cold winter evening he had just come in from buying some groceries at the nearby corner shop. It had been a struggle to walk even that small distance. He sat down in his armchair next to the gas fire to get his breath back. He thought about this childhood when he and his companions roamed the hillsides; how strong and vigorous he had been then. He thought of the love and warmth of his parents' house. If only he could relive those days. With his mind full of these memories he drifted into his final sleep.

The police kicked the door of his flat in a few weeks later.
'It's in here Sarge,' said the young impressionable constable, visibly shaken.
'Imagine dying all alone and unmissed like that Sarge,' he said as they waited for the body to be removed. 'It's terrible.'
'It happens, son, it happens,' replied the more sanguine older man.
'I wonder what kind of a life he had. Did anyone ever care for him? But we'll never know now, eh, Sarge?'

Geraldine Horan

Geraldine was born in London of Irish parents. She attended Catholic Convent School and after taking her examinations travelled through Europe and the Near East teaching English. On her return to London she worked in Publishing, Radio, TV & Film. She started to write 6 years ago working on a film adaptation of John B. Keanne's Big Maggie, after which she took a video course and attended scriptwriting courses at Birkbeck College, University of London. Since joining Women's Ink 2 years ago she has started to write short stories and TV comedy scripts.

PSYCHO-KILLERS, ROSE GARDENS AND TV

She had always thought herself a sensible down to earth type of person, our Mrs. Bramble. Warm woollies in winter and Clarke airtex shoes in summer, you know the ones, with sponge insoles 'Comfort More Than Speed.'

She had married her childhood sweetheart Arthur Bramble at the suitable age of 21 years and they had been together for forty uneventful ones, producing two unassuming children. They bought their first and last house in Chatham Kent, (as Arthur had worked in the shipyards), alternating between families at Christmas and had two weeks summer holiday in Bournemouth every year. All had gone according to plan yes, Frieda thought she was a very lucky woman, no unexpected or unforeseen event had touched their lives, until .....

One morning as she tended her garden, pruning her prized Queen Elizabeth roses a strange woman all big hair, bosom and lip gloss, seemed to be attacking her with a long furry, funnel-shaped object, which turned out to be a microphone.
'Did you know him, Mrs. Bramble, just to say 'Good Morning'or REALLY KNOW HIM, what he was REALLY like?'
Mrs. Bramble dropped her secateurs, mesmerized by all the frantic action. Cameras, microphones, bossy women, energetic young men dragging heavy equipment with a mire of trailing wires, all trying to get into her house!
'Where do you think you're going with those mucky boots?'
Mrs. Lipgloss suddenly shouted, 'Cut!'
Turning on a positively bucket-wrenching smile and with outstretched hand she ingratiated her way into Mrs. Bramble's living room, ushering her lackeys back into the garden. Louise

Bantrum, alias Mrs. Lipgloss, explained to Mrs. Bramble that her next door neighbour, the nice young Paul Maplethorpe, was in fact a homicidal mass murder. He preyed on under-age homosexual boys with no fixed abode, whom he duly dismembered and buried in his back garden. Mrs. Bramble, stunned by this news, mumbled,

'Always a keen gardener, our Paul.'

'Well yes, quite, Mrs. Bramble, what we need is someone who really knew him, what he was like as a neighbour, you know the sort of thing, hobbies, well perhaps not that - did you like him?' Mrs. Bramble sank into her comfy chintz armchair, still reeling from this horrendous revelation, remembering all the teas and recipes they had shared. She shuddered at the thought of his steak and kidney pies! Louise was unstoppable, ignoring Mrs. Bramble's obvious distress she uttered the phrase that was to change Frieda's life forever.

'It could be worth 'A LOT OF MONEY' and Frieda don't worry about all those dreadful chequebook journalists and nasty newspaper editors, I'll protect you and...'

'What did you say, 'A LOT OF MONEY?'

Frieda awoke from her ghastly trance, 'How much is 'A LOT' Mrs. Lip ... I mean Louise?'

'We're talking six figures.'

The two women's eyes met and they immediately knew that a deal had been struck.

Frieda or Freddie Bramble as she became known spent the next year on every TV, Satellite and Radio programme, appearing in all the National Dailies, Sundays, Local Newspapers and Women's Magazines. She was an overnight success. Everyone loved her seemingly innocent, yet ghoulish stories of her friendship with the "Gay Serial Killer". She never tired of recounting how Paul would proudly polish his collection of skulls, noting that they would be worth a fortune one day.

Asked whether this seemed a little odd to her? She promptly replied, 'Everyone has to have a hobby, don't they?' and smiled sweetly.

Louise and Freddie became firm friends or perhaps conspirators. Louise masterminded Frieda's transformation into "Freddie". Freddie took to wearing sharp little Chanel suits, accessorised with tasteful gilt jewellery, a short neat bob hair style, discreetly highlighted, completed the visual metamorphous. Freddie's tastes changed dramatically too, she no longer drank Port and lemon or cheap sherry on a Friday night with Arthur but preferred champagne with Louise at the various celebrity parties they both attended. Chatham the suburban backwater offered Freddie no stimulus for her increasing appetites, both mental and physical. She was not adverse to a young man's steely thigh or tight buttock and found that they reciprocated her attentions. Freddie seemed to thrive in her found environment far removed from her past humdrum existence.

She did return to Arthur in Chatham for brief overnight stops when she wittered on about whom she had met and the latest gossip in her glamorous "New World." Arthur would sit by the fire smoking his pipe watching TV ignoring every syllable she uttered but politely nodding and making suitable grunts when called for. On one such evening Freddie failed to notice that Arthur had suffered a heart attack and was not even making his usual noises. She was of course heart-broken, but mentioned, 'I knew that pipe would be the end of him.'

With Arthur gone and the children grown up and living God knows where, Louise suggested that she move to London and stay with her until she found her feet. By now Louise was no longer the hungry regional reporter but Freddie's agent, gone was the tarty glamour, replaced by plain no nonsense business practicality, bordering on dowdy. As Freddie became ever more successful and famous she acquired a polished predatory sexuality that attracted numerous waifs and strays including Louise's boyfriend Archie, an out of work actor who fell hopelessly in love with the aging carnivore. Freddie treated men like slaves and disposed of them if they displeased her, Archie at the moment, pleased her.

Louise seemingly oblivious to the relationship continued to work long hours calculating extortionate royalties and commissions on Freddie's numerous business ventures, while deducting a massive fifty percent fee for her trouble. She had reconciled these deductions as 'Dues,' my God had she earnt them! She had often thought that Freddie was a cross-fertilization of 'Attila the Hun' and 'Lucretia Borga' - and unfortunately alive. Louise only had herself to blame for creating this Frankensteinesque monster, she had taught Freddie all she knew and together they had capitalised on every situation, until eventually Freddie had her own 'Chat Show', now Freddie was the celebrity.

Louise eventually had a penthouse office set up in Canary Wharf, so Freddie could breeze in and out shouting obscenities at all the staff. Louise knew this would please her immensely and also serve as a diversion away from her dubious business practices.

All was rosy in the garden until one day ....

Freddie decided to breeze into the office before leaving for a weekend in Paris with Archie. Mowing down a couple of secretaries and barging past the receptionist, who apparently didn't recognize her after her umpteenth facelift, she crashed into Louise's office.

'Money, Louise, I need a bloody great suitcase of Lucre.'
Louise, haggard and half cut, looked up from her computer.
'Yes, of course, Oh Mighty One - how much?'
Freddie grabbed her handbag which fell to the floor emptying the contents. The two women grappled on the floor picking up the pieces, unfortunately, Freddie picked up Louise's bank statements, her newly acquired facelift nearly fell to the floor.
'How the hell did you manage that?'
Louise staggered to her feet and attempted to straighten her gabardine skirt, which by this point was halfway up her waist.
'Simple, I don't spend money on other people's useless boyfriends, facelifts, Oh yes and the monkey gland transfusions - hick'

Freddie was still kneeling on the floor clasping the incriminating statements incredulously. Through immaculately capped clenched teeth she managed to hiss
'They're hormonal shots ... and I told you under no circumstances were you ...'
'Yeah. Yeah. We know.'

Freddie took a closer inspection of the statements and slowly the picture emerged. The one million pounds sterling balance was made up by a whopping 50% commission that Louise had been deducting from all the contracts that they had signed.
'You've been robbing me blind.'
Louise realised through her alcoholic haze that this was serious.
'You owe me.'
'Not THAT much I don't! Clear your desk, if you can, - then I'll call the police.'

The two women looked at one another like prize fighters before the contest, each eyeing the opponent waiting and watching for a sign, a glimmer. No words were spoken until Freddie turned to Louise as she staggered out the door under her bundle of files. 'It was 'A LOT OF MONEY' Louise.'

SHADES OF AMBER

Standing on a corner, shouting, shaking or being shaken? Anger, red face, exploding. Desire, lust, lies. Traffic screeches. Knowing without proof, evidence or validation. Shocked faces glide by, what were they to me. Cheap bluff. Amateur. *Remembering ....*

Hot, long-drawl, airport drive. Cool breezes like floating muslin sway up from the lake. Tall but tall buildings, red brick gangsteresque blocks that mingle with elegant glass fibrous concoctions, above the rattle of the antiquated train station. Virile winding river twisting through the heart of the city, under the quaint humped-back bridges.

Dizzy, like a juiced-up cocktail. Flaying arms, violence. Blow to elbow - highest point of anatomy. Oh! ... Slap that ridiculous face - missed! Presents snatched. back. Malicious smile curls across that face. Return expression, cross road. Clouds open. Turning my head skyward I drink absolution. *Seeing .....*

Smart Chicago-chic cocktail bars with Oscar- winning waiters fill her head. Impossibly perfect, manicured women, screely voices, pivotal vision, scan the expensive restaurants and bars for their prey. Younger versions accompany these surgically enhanced vampires on their mission throughout the windy city.

The night, singing like a nightingale, sweet, fragile, amusing, he like a tiger insight of his prey, smiling, sickly knowing smile, acquiesces to my every whim. Bribes, tantalise, eau de parfume, champagne, sumptuous supper. Gentle, bustling bars, happy

faces, miss- matched couple. Escape. ......
but then .....

Red and white checked table clothes dotted the small park by the lake. The orchestra filled the night air. Bernstein danced above the captive audience, mingling with the smell of barbecued chicken and the pop of uncorked Californian Chardonnay. As the rosy twilight descended, candles were lit, the happy couple walked through the American dream incarnate.

Ping Pong, bat ball, flippant sincerity. Was he 'Stupid?' - not care - the latter. Ambling out of bar, chiding, quarrelsome, two old adversaries moving onto the next venue. Fashionable restaurant, yum, yum oysters, champagne, pink lamb cutlets, chocolate confections, delicious syrupy liquors. Red wine splashing across pristine white tablecloth. Immediately replaced, over-attentive waiter. Gets jealous, moves closer, rejection, laughs, orders bill - taxi.
Driving down .....

Magnificently, tree-lined avenues, home to American- styled bookshops, coffee bars, designer shops, stylish restaurants. The black taxi driver tells them about 'Downtown Blues Bars', she longs for 'Downtown' music, edge, danger, people who do not wear GAP. They never get 'Downtown' ever, no, not really.

Leaving restaurant, jibes about hair, plan escape. Fall into taxi - fall out of taxi. Oh! no!! - he is still there! Not the agreement, reneged promises, protestations. Years of unspoken words like a volcanic eruption flood from my mouth. Accusations, abuse, a mutant diabolical tirade. Can't stop, won't stop, confessional, exhaustion, relief, the sweet stench of death, cleansed soul.

Then Again ... New York ...

Obviously, gay, handsome, hotel staff. Style conscious, sterile interiors, O.D'd neon signs. Walk - Don't Walk No shades of Amber. Checkmate - no escape licentious, unlicensed flirting. Suffocating in that New York hotel room, 'Drowning, not waving.' Eat, drink, everything too much. Bite on lip, try to forget. Air Hostess, eating with his eyes - Desperate. Lunch, Grand Central Station, Oyster Bar. Slow death in Paramount Hotel's 'Whiskey Bar.'
Leers, obvious - invisible. Expects quite death. Hate, disgust, like a cat bringing you dead prey. Did he want applause?

Turning the key in the door, I hear the radio play.
'I miss my man, but aim's gett'n better.'
Love that song. Answer machine plays pathetic messages. He thinks silence is poignant, yawn. Costs him nothing, risks nothing, gives nothing. 'Take what you can, while you can' is his doctrine. Operating on the negative, lowest common denominators.

He is like a very thin volume that took a long time to read. Predictable, instantly forgettable, Chinese take-away. Paper thin, when you wanted solid gold or even just a shade of Amber?

TURNING

She takes his arm and says,
'I love you'
He turns away.

She takes his arm and says,
'I need you'
He turns away.

She takes his arm and says,
'I want you'
He turns and says 'Hey'

He takes her arm and says
'I want you'
She turns away.

He takes her arm and says
'I need you'
She turns away.

He takes her arm and says
'I love you'
She turns and says 'That'll Be The Day'

Yvonne Fisher

After training at the Webber - Douglas Academy of Dramatic Art, Yvonne Fisher had a lot of repertory and touring experience playing many leading and character parts. She then decided to train as a teacher and studied at Birmingham and taught Drama and English for nearly 20 years in London Schools.

She also concentrated on her third interest writing and had some small success. When she was 18 years old she wrote a series of articles for the Daily mirror called 'Stop and Think.' Recently she has some TV work and played parts such as the clairvoyant Aunt in 'Anything can Happen,' for Children's TV and the Gypsy in 'Jonathon Mead Show,' plus as eccentric footballer fan in a world cup advert for Snickers Chocolate Bar.

WATERS OF THE PAST

One evening when I was correcting Class 3 homework, there was a ring at the door and a woman who had lived next door to us during my schooldays was standing there. I remembered her as Mrs Smith.

My family and hers had played a sort of non-musical chairs with each other and she now lived in a house where my parents had occupied a flat when I was very young.

'This is Mr Jones who has a connection with the flood you were in as a child,' she said bringing forward a dark-haired man with deep-set rather piercing eyes. 'He wants to see the people who were around when it happened, so I brought him to visit you. I hope you don't mind. He has just come from Canada, and hasn't been in this country for years. Not since he lost someone in the flood.'

'It was my sister,' said the man. 'She was living in the bottom flat of Number 3.'

'Where you lived before me,' said Mrs Smith. 'I heard all about the tragic death of the girl when I moved there. People said that the father of the family had let the girl drown in the flat below.'

'You are talking about my father,' I burst out in horror. 'He never let her drown. He tried to make her hear. But, he got no answer when he knocked so he thought she was away.'

'It was in all the papers that the man had saved his family, but let the girl die,' said Mrs Smith.

'It was my sister,' said the man from Canada moving closer to me. I moved back under his sinister gaze.

'I was only five but I remember how it was, my father did his best to save her. We were all terrified,' I said as I remembered when I grew up at the age of five.

I remember clearly the day before the flood. My mother and I

and little brother had spent a lovely Sunday at Bushy Park.
'This is where the royal family spend a lot of time,' said my father. I looked around expecting to see Kings and Queens appear through the misted trees. 'We might even see the royal princesses.' Thoughts of long golden hair and sparkling coronets filled my mind, as later we went home on the top of a bus. The red and gold sunset tipped the trees as we travelled back to Fulham and what was in store for us.

Home in the flat and it was time for bed.
'Must I sleep in this thing, Mummy?' I complained looking at the railed cot - too big for a baby and too babyish for a girl of five.
'Don't be silly, you know you are having a new bed. It's only for tonight, the dustman took your old bed away this morning.'
'Alright,' I was too tired to argue and once in bed was soon away.

I woke from a hazy depth of sleep to feel my father shaking my shoulder.
'Get up! Get up!' he urged me. 'Go and knock on that door up there.' He pointed to a trap door in the ceiling, which led to the flat upstairs. I was shy.
'I don't like to,' I cried.
'You must!' said my father, 'there is a flood and we will all be drowned. We must get upstairs.' He pulled down the metal steps and up I went. My heart was beating loudly and my face felt hot and embarrassed. What would the woman think? We hardly knew her. I knocked.
'Louder, Louder, you must make her hear!'
My hands hurt as I knocked. My father was speaking to my mother, 'Take the baby and I will go and see if the girl downstairs is in.' I knocked and knocked and eventually a sleepy voice said, 'What do you want?'

My father was back and saying to my mother. 'I can't make her hear. She must be away. She often is at weekends. I'll try again.' By the time he came upstairs, we were settling down for a night of waiting and watching in a strange flat, high above the water. I was sitting in a chair facing a slopping window. I looked out. I could see no water but I could hear it.

I remember nothing after this till I was on a train with Dad, having gradually recalled, spent a shy couple of nights with the neighbour. We were on our way to join my mother and brother in Sussex, where they were staying with my Aunt and Uncle.
'It is your birthday soon,' said my father as we came out of the dark tunnel, which always scared me when I took this journey. 'I've got a diary for you. It is a good time for you to start writing in it. I always keep one myself. Then you've got a record of all that has happened.'
The idea of a diary jerked my thoughts back to the present.
If I could find my dad's diary, then I would have proof that he had not let the girl die as the man from Canada had thought.

I looked everywhere among the furniture that had been in the family for years. I rang my cousin who said, 'Look in that old desk of your fathers. I remember him keeping some notebooks there.' My cousin, with whom I had been brought up, had a better memory about our early life that I had. Sure enough I found the diary there. I flicked through it until I came to the date I was looking for. There was my father's handwriting….
'Tried again to make the girl downstairs hear. Must get the family to safety. Came down once more but still no answer. She must be away... Have to go back now as the water is rising'.

While I had been looking for the diary, Mr Smith from Canada had crossed my path often. At the tube station in the morning, and at the window of the neighbours where he was staying, he waved at me. Then I came upon him in the station buffet.

'May I join you?' he asked, bringing his coffee. I thought his smile seemed sinister. I wouldn't mention the diary till I had found it.

Then when I actually found it I had not come across him for weeks. I felt somehow disappointed. I did want to clear the matter up. Was it that I hated the thought of his disapproval? No, of course not. I hated the injustice that he was doing to my father.

Then one evening the doorbell rang and he was there.

'Do come in,' I greeted him. 'I meant to say something to you the other day, but thought the time wasn't right.'

'Now it is?' he asked.

'Yes, I have found my father's diary.' I opened the small oblong book and pointed at a page. 'There it is in my father's words. 'I couldn't make the girl hear."

But my visitor is looking at me, not at the book.

'I know all about what happened. I read the final reports in the papers. I soon realised that your father was innocent. That he had tried his best to rescue my sister.'

'Then why have you been haunting me?' I was on the verge of tears.

He came closer, 'I just wanted to get to know you.'

He smiled and took my hand, and he did not look sinister at all.

Angel Strand

Angel is a pseudonym. The writer was a founder member of Wednesday Women and still continues to love the idea of a supportive network of creative women writers. She is grateful that other people now do the work needed to put the idea into practice!

THE PARENTAL HUM
(an extract from a novel in progress)

Background:
In 1976, when Liz is 21, the laws governing adoption change. But it isn't until her early 30s that she begins the long road home to her birth relatives. She is living with an alcoholic sax-player, Danny.
She finds her birth mother, Rita, a singer who gives her a photograph of herself and one of Liz as an infant. In the following excerpt Liz has decided to tell her adoptive parents and is visiting them for Sunday lunch. Liz is called 'Lou' by her sister, Jackie.

A note on the writing process: This extract didn't begin life as an extract, but as the first germ of a novel. Consequently, its changes have been as many as if it were a person who has been growing up and outwards for a while.

*

Liz watched Iris hold the Sunday joint aloft on the meat fork - so that the fat dripped back nice, into the pan with the potatoes. Blood oozed at the prongs of the fork as Iris cut into the flesh and put a proper portion on five best green dinner plates and a bowl laid out on the kitchen table.

The spring sunlight struggled through the steamy kitchen windows and formed a halo in Iris' newly-permed hair. The dyed, dense, black curls were tinged with fire. 'Now' she said, pointing with the tip of her carving knife to one of the plates. 'That's you. Is that enough?'

Liz looked at the plate that was her and nodded. She was thinking about what she had to say and how to say it, the words felt like concrete in her stomach and the food on the table looked abstract. It wasn't easy to get a word in. The parents went on droning about their lives, telling her what the council were doing, the neighbours, the relatives in Ilford. The parental hum. It was much easier to listen to it than say anything that mattered. But she had to.

'Right' said Iris, pointing to the plates one by one, this time with the dull green potato spoon. 'Right. That's William, that's Jack. That's Ben and that's the Baby. She does remind me of William's mother. She really does. She's definitely our side of the family. There's nothing of Ben's side in her.' Ben had schizophrenia in the family, so that was a relief. Iris looked straight at Liz. 'Jackie tried everything she could to breastfeed her, you know. Ben even bought her a nipple pump, one of those things you stick on...' she clawed her own breast. 'And now she's got the varicose veins.' She grasped the handle of the vegetable saucepan. 'The baby says Grandad now,' she shrieked as a cloud of vegetable steam enveloped her head. 'He's everso pleased!'

The kitchen door was too big for its frame now. It was stiff these days. It needed a good push. Just like him. His mind was good though. Forty years of marriage had conditioned him to know when he was being talked about. William popped his head in. 'What would you like to drink with your dinner, Liz?' he asked.

Liz opened her mouth to answer.

'I was just telling Liz about the baby saying Grandad, Will!' said Iris and she spun round with the vegetable spoon in her hand. A tiny speck of boiled brussel landed on his cardigan.

'Watch it!' he barked.

Iris made a face at him...

He ignored her. 'I just heard your song, Liz, on the wireless.'
'What song?' asked Iris, ladling the greens.
'Catch a falling star...' his voice lilted although did not sing. He couldn't sing.
'Oooh,' squealed Iris. 'I remember that! You didn't speak for a whole year after we got you. I thought you were tongue-tied. And then one day we had the radio on and that song came on and you sang it - Catch a falling star and put it in your pocket - the whole thing. We looked at you in astonishment, didn't we Will!?'
'Ha, ha, ha.' Will's dentures slipped as he remembered. He half remembered. His version was a little different but he didn't say so..

Why now? Liz wondered. Why should that come on the radio and they are talking about it, yet again. Why had she sung it? Maybe Rita had sung it to her. She had a beautiful voice. She wanted to say it, right now. But it was so HARD! I know who my mum is. I… she would have to interrupt the hum and send a bombshell into their lives. They knew bombshells. They had lived through the war.

'It got embarrassing in the end' Iris waved the tinned carrots. 'D'you remember that holiday camp, Will!?'
Will opened his mouth to speak. But to no avail. It was a rhetorical question.
'I wanted the ground to open up and swallow me. I really did. I'd left you on the beach, Liz,' she wailed. 'You loved the beach. You used to spend hours playing on your own. I thought, I'll just nip across and see the tiny tots talent contest.
'So I was sat there in the auditorium and all these lovely little girls came on, their hair all nice and clean and lovely dresses. And then on walked this urchin, absolutely filthy, all covered in sand, singing COMPLETELY out of tune. I thought Christ!

And then it dawned on me it was you! I really wanted the floor to open up and swallow me.' Iris hit the plate in front of her with the spoon and carrots tumbled, onto the china.

Liz lit a cigarette and suddenly, involuntarily, spun back in her mind to Danny in bed last night wanting anal sex.
She looked up from her nails and saw her father sniggering at the story. Her blood boiled inside her. I sang, she thought clearly, because I wasn't the child of your fucking imagination. I sang because my mother was a singer and I was born that way. You should have encouraged my voice, encouraged me. The anger was so furious she was scared that if she tried to speak she would kill them. She opened her mouth. Her heart pounded but she could not find the words. And then the back door lurched open.

Sunlight and rainbows burst in, in the van of the clucking, squealing Baby, in its wheeled chariot, pushed by its own mother.
'Oooh, ooh, ooh. Get out of my way William.' shrieked Iris. 'Dindins nearly ready! How's my Baby?' She looked at the last carrot in the saucepan, hesitated, and threw the little phallic shape, water and all, at her husband's plate.
'Cap 'andies then, cap 'andies.' sang Will, patting his gentle hands together.
The Baby imitated him, laughing.
'That's William, that's Ben, that's Jackie, that's the Baby. And that's you Liz.' shrieked Iris. 'All right?'
'Helloooo!' sang Jackie, as she trundled in. She wore a cheap skirt in a high street colour and a sleeveless blouse that ejected its interfacing progressively with each step she took. The cut of her shoes revealed her toes' cleavage. 'All right Lou!?' she said and docked on one hip, her hands falling limply by her sides.

Liz sat up straight, assuming the fit posture of unruly changeling in the presence of the real daughter of the house, the heir. Her little sister was beautiful, she thought. She really did have eyes like dark diamonds, cheekbones curving moon-crescently and pale with glimmer shine on a delicate sprinkling of freckles. Her hair was a mane of dark lustre. It glinted around her heart-shaped face. She was blooming. Must be motherhood. Ben's deep voice echoed behind her. 'All right?' he asked of the room in general. 'All right!?'

'Now,' screeched Iris. 'In the dining room, all of you. I don't want dinner to get cold.'

'Jackie, now look. This is you.'

Jackie's diamond eyes searched the plate for herself.

'Oh.' she said. 'Best plates.'

'And that's Ben and that's the Baby.' Iris moved close to her natural daughter. 'That's Liz and that's Daddy.' she said.

Will ignored his mundane little metamorphoses on the plate and, taking up the bottle of Lambrusco, he led a higgledy piggledy dance into the dining room.Through the kitchen doorway they went, through the dining room arch. And as they went, they left themselves on their plates and became their table manners. They all sat down. The plates were rushed in, one by one, by Iris, who wanted no help whatsoever.

And William became the Slow Eater, whose methodical chewing was as unstoppable as Time itself. Jackie was the Fussy One. She picked. Lately, of course, she had become the New Mother as well. She spooned the Baby nicely in the Fussy One's bored gaps. It suited her. She was Rounded at last.

The Baby was Delight but it was universally agreed that she was on the verge of becoming Chaos and needed to be kept an eye on... Ben was the Universal Son-in-Law and his plate was piled high in recognition of his young manhood, his labours and the seeding of the family line.

Liz was the Wolf. She consumed everything that was put in front of her. What's more she never put on an ounce, while the other women in the family only had to look at a food cupboard and they put on half a stone. Hummmm. No-one begrudged her the food. At least this Wolf was not at the door. She had a roof over her head. The Fates were appeased.

Iris was the Martyr. She didn't like a meal. She only cooked one because he liked one.

'Aren't you having any carrots, Iris?' asked The Slow Eater.

'I'm not over fond of carrots,' said the Martyr, softly.

'Oh? I thought you liked carrots.' he continued.

The Martyr gave him a filthy look. 'There weren't enough. Satisfied?'

'Weren't enough?!' he scoffed. 'Why not?'

'Look, never mind. Just eat your dinners, all of you. Never mind me.'

Guilt descended, particularly on the Universal Son-in-Law who had the most and, because he was a lad with a conscience, knew he should be very grateful for her hospitality.

The fussy New Mother, being recently martyred herself, laid back in her chair and encouraged the Baby to eat.

The Slow Eater chewed mismanagement along with his meat. He knew there was no reason for it. He had become used to it. The best thing to do was say a prayer in your heart. The meal continued in silence. When they did speak their voices seemed small. Someone, way back in the mists of time, had taught the elders that it was bad manners to talk at table. Liz thought about bringing out her photographs... She could see them dancing across the table singing... the world is a stage, the stage is a world of entertai - ai - nment! She killed the thought.

The Martyr and the Fussy New Mother drifted away from the table, dragging their manners behind them. The Son-in-Law followed to have a fag with his wife.

Liz kept her father company while he finished his dinner. It would be perfect to tell just him, she thought, as he chewed. He'd understand. He'd be curious. She could trust him a bit, her dad. It was him who had been loving, consistently. But her dad was wrapped in a taboo. He was a lot older than anyone, for a start. He was a boy, somebody else's husband. And people choked on their dinners if you gave them a shock. They had to be rushed to hospital. Look at the Queen Mother.

Iris burst in, looked at The Slow Eater's plate, grabbed the salt and pepper pots, the pickles, the mustard he liked on his dinner. She went back into the kitchen, leaving the dining room door open, which meant she was coming back. He slowly continued his dinner, despite the draught of her disapproval.

Liz got up and closed the door again. She had to. She had to. She prayed too that he would soon finish. It worked. He placed his knife and fork together and took up his napkin.

'I think Mum wants us to take the plates in' he said.

'Dad, I need to tell you something. I'm going to tell everyone after lunch. I've traced my birth mother.'

He looked at her. His eyes were a little rheumy. 'Good for you, Liz. Oh that is wonderful.'

'I have some photographs.' she said.

'Oh jolly good. Let's go into the lounge and we'll all look at them.' He took his plate and went into the kitchen where the The Martyr had made tea.

'Liz has got something to show us' he said.

'What?' she said as she carried the tray behind him into the lounge. 'What?'

In the lounge everyone sat on the Dralon comfies, except Jackie, who was on the floor with Baby. The Martyr perched herself on top of the leatherette pouffe that sloped. The china cups clinked on the tray on the rug as everyone helped themselves. Ben accidentally took William's cup but William said it didn't matter. Iris started to protest but then let it go. They were both men after all.

'I have some news,' said Liz, 'I've traced my birth mother.' She was very careful to say the politically correct 'birth' instead of just saying my mother, or my natural mother or, heaven forbid, my real mother.

'You've got some photographs of your mother, eh Liz?' he said. Iris looked daggers at William.

'I'm her mother. Did you know about this?'

'Just now. Liz just told me, in the dining room.' he said, defensively.

'She was a singer.' said Liz, triumphantly. 'I do have photos if you'd like to see them.'

'Yes' said William 'Let's see. I thought she was a laundress.' Liz held out the picture of her mother to William. She was proud. Rita was beautiful.

'Oh yes,' said William, 'Oh yes. You can see the likeness.'

'Yes.' said Iris.

Liz gingerly held out the picture of a fat, happy, laughing baby, about nine months old, to Iris.

'That's my baby!' cried Iris and her eyes shone.

Jackie was the last to look at the baby picture and she wept quietly. Her own Baby, seeing its mother's tears, took up the wail.

'There, there.' said Iris. 'Here. Give the picture back to Liz, go on. Take it to Liz.' And she put the picture into the little paw with dinner on it. The Baby took the photograph, looked at it, and said 'Abbab.'

And because she was such a clever Baby she got a whoop of joy from everyone for the sheer brilliance of her words. Brightening, she toddled across the carpet towards Liz with the photograph. Liz caught her with a firm, loving grasp and scooped her up in the air. The Baby laughed and laughed.

Ingrid Curry

Ingrid was born in Sweden. She lives in London, where she works as a teacher and translator. This contribution is an extract from a novel Ingrid is working on at present.

PICA PICA
(Extracts from a novel - work in progress)

Chapter 15

The small flat gave little space for big parties, but Hannah's parents were known for their hospitality and generous spreads. The crowdedness seemed to Hannah to add to the warmth, providing the very essence of the joviality.

On the occasion of her father's birthday, Hannah had insisted on wearing her sky blue taffeta dress despite her mother's protestations that this was not an important birthday and hence it did not demand such grand clothing. Hannah had pleaded with her mother, who had relented and she stood, small and groomed, lightly turning her body inside her dress in order to make the crisp taffeta crackle and foam. Its fragile blueness shifted in nuance in the reflection of the living room chandelier and the high candles which flickered on the dining table in readiness for burly men of good appetites and finely fashioned women, who would be glad of the caressing light on their pale winter complexions.

The supper was enjoyed in a mood of sounding crystal brimming with icy vodka, sipped in fulfilment and laughter. Short speeches interspersed the dishes her mother carried in to noisy acclaim. Hannah was helping by serving the bread, but as this was the first evening party she was allowed to attend, she also had the honour of sitting next to her father. Wrapped in his tender presence and the reflected homage her father was paid, as the birthday celebrant, Hannah perceived the evening as full of mellowness and pride.

In waiting for the table to be cleared away and the card table to be erected, the guests crowded into the hall and spilled over into the master bedroom. Hannah found herself in the middle of the assembled party pressed against her parents' bedstead. Her uncles and aunts were standing tall around her, smoking and joking, sometimes lowering their voices in order to blanket a particularly risqué punch line from her young ears. Hannah loved the grown-up talk even if she didn't understand the topics discussed. She moved in the darkened sound, soaked with contentment, pleased to be benignly ignored in her private world.

It was at this time, shrouded in the noisy collective of all her favourite adult people that Hannah first heard of her future inheritance.

'It's ridiculous,' a man's voice said, 'the child is only seven! And what about the woman herself?'

'Surely she is still too young to give her possessions away. What is behind it all? I don't understand.'

Hannah pricked up her ears at the sound of the word 'child', and began to listen actively. A child of seven was not usually a subject for the witty festive crowd around her. She felt it might concern her - even if she was eight.

Her Uncle Paul looked down to her, stroking her hair:

'Little heiress, aren't you! Now, who would have believed it?'

Hannah looked up into his smiling face, trying to read any understanding into his words. She refrained from asking him what 'heiress' meant, feeling it might be dangerous to reveal such childish ignorance, but also unwilling to cause the topic to change before she had tried to glean any form of meaning from their talk. But then she saw her mother's face. It bore an expression she had learnt to fear and at best respect. Her mother was clearly angry. Hannah thought desperately of how she could have caused such anger on such a happy occasion. It came as a great relief to her when she realised that her mother's anger was not directed at her - but at her uncle.

Her mother was furious with her own brother:
'Paul, this is not the place!' her voice was a lash of retribution. Hannah had never seen such overt anger being directed towards any of her mother's brothers and sisters. She stood transfixed trying not to disturb the vibrations of emotions, in order to find out at first hand why she had become the focus of interest and so much turbulence. She feared from experience that later, upon asking, she would get the child's version lacking all adult spicing and general elements of the truth.

However, there was no more to be revealed. Hannah's mother's stern look and whipping whisper had silenced her uncle and he had followed her mother back into the room for a prominent position at the poker table, where the subjects of conversation were again whirling among the participants like multicoloured scarves drawn out of magicians' hats. All anger lines were smoothed away from her mother's face as her hostess voice invited Paul to start dealing and he in turn rewarded her with a grin of understanding and complicity.

Hannah resigned herself to the fact that no more information would ensue on any serious subject that night. The gathered family had assumed their patter and well-conspired lightheartedness. She would have to start her quest another day, she thought climbing up onto her father's lap as he ordered his cards. They turned into a busted flush.
'Give me luck, Goldilocks, give me strength, this is some awful start!' her father smiled, giving her his counters to pile into pillars of varied colours and heights.
'Some start, Daddy, some start', she answered promising herself not to forget to find out about the seven year old heiress. I will ask Daddy she thought and squeezed his hand for luck as he

began the bidding.

Chapter 16

Hannah asked her father the day after his birthday. Her mother was at a friend's house playing bridge, which was a regular monthly event. On these evenings Hannah and her father usually did something special before she went to bed. They would play Ludo or go to visit her grandfather. Her father would sometimes bring home magazines and they would read the cartoons together. There was always something extra good for supper and Hannah would be allowed to stay up a little later than usual. This evening, due to the late night before, they had decided to stay in.

Hannah's mother had left them a luxurious tray, with lace napkins, fine china and a platter of leftovers from the party. They feasted on cold seafood omelette, Russian salad, smoked eel, cream cheese and, especially for Hannah, finely sliced cucumber in parsley dressing. They ate their supper with small white rolls and salty butter. For dessert they enjoyed thin wedges of marzipan gateau and almond biscuits. Hannah sat at the coffee table propped up in a deep armchair eating her supper with the great solemnity she felt the occasion demanded. After their meal, her father went out into the kitchen and made them both a cup of tea, which Hannah drank amber-clear with a spoonful of honey, while her father would stir in a trace of cream in his darker brew.

'It's like another birthday party, daddy,' she said.

'Aren't I the lucky one! To be having two parties, Don't you think?' he answered.

'Yes, you are,' she replied, and after a while she added:

'What shall we do now?'

'Right, what about patience?'

Hannah thought for a moment before answering.

'I would like to play poker, daddy.'

Her father laughed out loud.

'Oh, you would, would you! Well, well - I don't know, you didn't bring me any luck yesterday, did you? I lost, didn't I? I lost all my counters, Hannikins.'

'I tried daddy,' she defended herself, feeling uncertain of the degree of responsibility allotted to her.

'Sweetheart Hannikins, I'm just joking. Come give me a kiss.'

She climbed up onto his lap nudging his face, as he stretched to reach a drawer at the table to take out a pack of cards.

'Here', he said, 'start dealing!'

Solemnly she began dealing, laying the cards very deliberately on the table in front of them.

'Good girl,' he said, 'one should never show the cards. You are doing very well.'

Hannah picked up the cards, trying to hold them away from her father's eyes, as he playfully tried to catch sight of her hand. This was difficult as she was sitting on his lap.

Hannah's heart took a leap as she looked at her cards. She had a beautiful hand. She sat up, eager to get the game going.

'I start then, as you dealt,' said her father.

'Right.'

'Two cards, please.'

'One, two,' she counted, looking up at him, 'more?'

'No, you can only buy once. Now it's your turn.'

'None!' she said, pink with excitement at her good fortune.

'I bet you are bluffing! Are your cards that good!'

'They are, daddy, they are.'

'Ah little Hannikins, the first rule in poker is having a poker face! When you are pleased you should look really miserable,' he pulled a long forlorn face, at which Hannah started laughing, dropping her cards on the floor.

'Yes, and did I forget to say that the second most important thing is not to drop your cards. Now - get yourself in order and let's play. I feel I might win. I bet you a cinema ticket that my cards are better than yours.'

'I see you,' said Hannah, holding her cards close to her chest. 'With what may I ask?'

'A cinema ticket, like you.'

'And where is it then?'

'You didn't have one either.'

'Oh silly me, I forgot, here you are.' He put an old bus ticket on the table. 'One cinema ticket.'

'It's not!'

'It is. It's a magic ticket, bus 51, it's 'Gone with the wind' all the way to the Roxy.'

Hannah shrieked with laughter,

'... and what will the man at the cinema say, when you show him an old bus ticket?'

'He will say,' he stood up now, straight as a soldier, 'enter My Lord and Princess of all spades and clubs, Queen of hearts and Heiress to all the diamonds!'

Hannah stopped laughing, he had said it, he had said 'heiress.' That word. She forgot her perfect poker hand, put her cards down in her lap and said without guarding her tongue:

'What is an heiress, daddy?'

He answered without the anger and hesitation she had expected: 'Someone who inherits, someone who gets something when someone is dead. When your mother's grandmother died, mother inherited the plates we have just eaten from. Now let's see your cards.'

Hannah showed her cards, but without her earlier joy and excitement.

'Heavens above, a Royal Straight Flush! Do you know it's only the second time in my life I have seen one.'

'When was the first time?'

'At the cinema, Popeye was playing Goofy and Donald Duck at the 'Muddy Boot Saloon', Popeye won.'

'Daddy!'

'Well, here is your ticket, Hannikins, you have won it squarely, now keep it safe, it's magic, remember. We will have a splendid time at the pictures.' He hadn't sensed her quietness, as she continued.

'Can children be heiresses, daddy?'

'Of course - well, girls -that is.'

'Not boys.'

'No, boys become heirs, but it's the same thing.' He looked up. 'Hannah why are you asking, sweetheart?'

'Uncle Paul said a girl - who was seven - was 'an heiress'.' Then, more deliberately, looking down at the discarded poker hand.

'He said I was 'an heiress' but he must be wrong because, they talked about 'an heiress' who was seven - and I am eight.'

Her father put his arms around her.

'I see', he said softly, 'Let me tell you all about it. Now sit back in your chair. Come little one.' He settled her back in the deep armchair, where she sat attentive and serious, looking at her father across the small table.

'Now,' he began, 'I have a cousin, in the country, by a large lake. She has a small cottage and she would like you to have it, when you are grown up. But - and this is unusual - she wants to give it to you now. She has asked me to look after it for you until you are twenty-one. That is all there is to it.'

'But where will she go?'

'Oh, she will stay in the house, but it will belong to you.'

'Has she no children?'

'No, she is on her own.'

'She must be lonely.'

'Well,' her father said thoughtfully, 'we might think so, we are always having so many people around us. People are different. I think she likes being on her own. And she has a dog and a cat, and... she has neighbours and...there are always the...

chickens!'

'Chickens!' Hannah was laughing again.

'Yes, chickens, you know … egg machines.' He flapped his elbows like bird wings making clucking noises.

'Daddy!' She started giggling.

'Hannikins, that's better, I'm a magician, I made you laugh again!'

Then seriously,

'I am so sorry you were worried. I should have told you earlier, I didn't think it mattered until you were older. I was wrong. But it's nice, don't you think, owning a little house. You are 'an heiress', despite the fact that you are eight! And what's more, your Uncle Paul was wrong, he meant no harm, but he should have shown you more respect'. He smiled at her. 'All right?'

'Yes. Is that why mother was cross with Uncle Paul?'

'Yes, she wanted to protect you.'

Hannah was stunned and in awe of the tone in which her father had spoken to her, addressing her in such an adult way. She felt honoured and full of love towards her father for the way he had treated her. It didn't matter that she didn't understand all the implication of her new situation. It didn't matter because she now had access to all the information she needed. When she wanted to, she could always ask again. There was no hurry she wasn't grown up yet.

'I see,' she said slowly, 'What is the cousin's name?'

'Martha.'

Chapter 17

Hannah's mother and father took her to see Martha when Hannah was 11 years old.

In the three years that had passed since Martha's first approach regarding her appointing Hannah as her heir, little had been said on the matter, at least to Hannah herself. Documents with black spidery letters had been received and Hannah's father had seen to having them copied before they were lodged in a large tin box where all the family's legal papers were kept.

Since her long conversation with her father, however, Hannah had taken these events calmly and with failing interest. Except for one occasion when a letter had arrived with the now familiar awkward writing and a Waterway Village postal mark, addressed to Hannah personally. Hannah had never received a letter before and sat quietly feeling grown up, stroking and smelling the envelope as if trying to sense the essence of the stranger, who seemed to have catapulted her into a future nobody could have foreseen.

Hannah's mother who sat at the kitchen table with her said:
'I know it is lovely to receive a letter, but it might be even more exciting to see what is inside. After all, an envelope is for everybody to touch, but what is inside is really private - for your eyes only. Shouldn't you open it?'
'Well, soon, I want to save it for later,' said Hannah.
'That's all right, let me know if you want any help with reading it,' said her mother and left her turning the letter in her hands.
After lunch, several hours after having received it, Hannah and her mother opened the letter. Hannah's mother brought a sculpted wooden letter opener from the desk in the living room and showed Hannah how to slit the letter by inserting the opener in the small open space at the corner of the envelope.

Hannah pulled out a small piece of lined paper and read:
'Dearest child, I haven't seen you since you were a little girl in a lacy bonnet and you must feel that you have never seen me! Do you wonder what I look like? Here is a photograph. Soon we will meet. Sincerely with best wishes. Your Aunt Martha.'
The photograph showed a wiry-haired woman cradling a white mongrel standing artlessly on a large flat rock by a stretch of

water. On the back was written: 'Martha and Raja on the Blue Mountain'.

Hannah smiled at the woman and nodded:

'Pleased to meet you Martha and Raja!'

She studied the photograph carefully. A lined face with light piercing eyes looked straight at the beholder as if challenged. What to, could not be understood or answered.

'Raja is an important name for such a scruffy looking dog,' said Hannah and touched the dog's nose.

'Martha always was a law unto herself,' said her mother.

'How do you mean,' said Hannah.

'Well,' said her mother,' she does what she likes, without asking other people or caring for their advice - always did.'

There was disapproval in her mother's voice Hannah detected. To Hannah growing up in an extended family where the slightest action and decision demanded far reaching debates and council, the idea of making up your own mind seemed adventurous and laced with spine-chilling excitement. She looked at the wild face in the windy barren landscape, sensing that the unfashioned hair was washed clean in stormy rains and flared in winds from grey waters.

Hannah dared a small point of disagreement.

'If she lives on her own, she has to do what she wants.'

'Don't argue, you don't understand how things have been for Martha - and that side of the family!' Her mother turned away having brought the exchange to a halt, she thought.

But Hannah was not so lightly dismissed. She had gained a grain of rebellion from her newfound distant relative and let the acuteness of the sharpened eyes in the photograph inject her with, until now, unfamiliar and, she feared, foolhardy courage. Willing to pay for it later - in the form of her mother's silent sullen disapproval - she ventured once more into the territory of dissent.

'I think she sounds brave and clever, to live alone and do things on her own, without anybody to ask.' Flushed with a new sense of power Hannah continued. 'I would like to be like her! Like Martha.'

Clutching her letter and the photograph she attempted a fast retreat into the living room, but was caught by her mother who held her in a fixed grip.
'Hannah, just you listen, you should not talk like that! Here everybody cares for you. You should be grateful, you are lucky, very lucky, to have such a family to care so much for you. You have everything a child could ask for. How dare you be so rude!'
'I am not rude.'
'It sounds like it. Like you don't know how good your life is. Martha is a strange woman. She has - a strange life.'
'I'm sorry, mother.'
Hannah understood what her mother meant, but felt sad her mother didn't understand her. Still, somewhere in the depth of her small unformed soul, she experienced a thrill, like a faint echo of otherness, which she found worthwhile protecting as she hugged herself together with the letter and photograph of Martha and Raja.

Now as she sat on the narrow gauge steam train, she was a little older, but the letter was still in her dress pocket. The photograph was thumbed and dog-eared and worn with frequent use and imagined encounters. Martha and Raja had become secret guides into a world of crooked routes and darkened mazes, where the unknown met the mysteries of those who did not act by consent and complicity.

The train chuffed through a beautiful midsummer landscape and Hannah and her parents ate their picnic and sipped coffee from flasks. At one long stop her father had jumped off the train and bought them all ice creams from a station-based kiosk, cheered on by Hannah and her mother, as they pretended the train would leave him behind. Hannah read the book of Greek sagas her father had given her and chatted with her parents. They were all happy and full of expectations. They were not used to long journeys and the trip was an adventure for them all. But to Hannah the real adventure was meeting her mentor.

But Martha was not at the station to meet them. Instead a man with a horse and cart, whom Hannah's father had known since childhood, was waiting for them. Hannah's parents muttered silently to themselves and it was easy to see that both of them were displeased. But then her father shrugged and turned to the man smiling with recognition.
'Meet Alfred!' he said and shook the man's hand. 'Alfred, good to see you!'
'Sure is. Good day to you.' Alfred touched his cap, grinned and invited them all to climb onboard.

Hannah was full of joy at the turn the trip had taken. As her father was talking to Alfred she listened to them, singing to herself as they scrambled along the forest-lined sandy road and sneaking a sideways look at her mother's less than happy face as the rickety, dusty cart had shattered her city-like creamy slickness into silly, overdressed inappropriateness.

As the forest cleared, the sun came out fully and shone on Hannah's future house. A small red cottage with white trimmings and a dilapidated veranda in an overgrown garden with a dog kennel, outside which a small, old and dirty dog was glaring at them. Raja was older than in her photograph. But Martha was nowhere to be seen.

Bernadette (Bernie) Donovan

Bernie was born and educated in Dublin. She came to London in the early sixties where she met and married Con. When her husband died in 1992 she rekindled her interest in writing, joining Wednesday Women's Writing Group. She has written many short stories, screenplays, and a novel for which she is still endeavouring to find a publisher.

PICNIC IN BELFAST

When I was growing up in Dublin we had very severe censorship. As teenagers my friends and I wasted an enormous amount of energy in endeavouring to obtain books on the Index, a list of books banned in Ireland. One such book was a love story by Kathleen Wilson. It was one of the most sensational novels of the forties. Everyone was talking about it and several copies had already been smuggled into Ireland. Much to our excitement my best friend Una obtained a copy whilst on holiday with her family in London.

'I had to smuggle it back in my knickers, in case my Mum found it,' she announced triumphantly. 'It's really hot stuff,' she added.

The book was quickly passed around our class of fourteen and fifteen year olds and by the time it reached me it was almost in tatters. It told of the adventures of a highly desirable, bosom-heaving young woman in the reign of Charles II. And the name of this classic - 'Forever Amber'. There were numerous bodice ripping and midnight trysts with my lady in her chamber.

Imagine our delight when Una arrived at the school on the last day of term with startling news.

'Guess what?' and not waiting for a reply rushed on, 'They have made a film of "Forever Amber."

'But it will be banned here,' I said. 'There isn't a chance of it getting shown, even if they cut out all the love scenes.'

'If they did that there wouldn't be five minutes left,' giggled Molly.

'I know that stupid, but my cousin who lives in Bangor said it's going to be on in Belfast next month,' Una answered with glee.

'Belfast!' we shouted in unison.

'How are we going to get permission to go to Belfast?' Bridget asked.

'And to a BANNED film,' Phil added.

We all lapsed into silence and then my evil mind began to work.
'You know how we will go picnicking once a week during the
hols. Well ... what's to stop us having a picnic in Belfast?' I
asked.

'Don't be daft, what do you think my Ma would say if I told her
we were going to Belfast for a picnic!' exploded Mary.

'We don't say we're going to Belfast. They rarely ask us where
we're going as they know we only go to Portmarnock or Bray.'

'But that's lying,' Mary continued.

'No it isn't, we just don't mention Belfast and anyone who
doesn't want to come can stay at home and we'll tell you all
about it when we get back,' I added maliciously.

No one murmured. There were six of us in our exclusive club
and we had borrowed our motto from the Three Musketeers
'One for all and all for one.'

'Do you know who's in it?' asked Kate.

'Yes,' replied Una, 'Linda Darnell is Amber and Cornel Wilde is
her lover AND George Sanders is Charles II.'

That clinched it. Those of us not in love with Cornel Wilde
were mad about George Sanders. We now had to work out our
plan of campaign for getting to Belfast. The next week was our
first picnic of the summer holidays. We deliberately set off early
in the morning and continued this routine for the next three
weeks so that when we were ready for our visit to Belfast our
families would not question our early start. There was a daily 9
o'clock train from Dublin nicknamed the 'smugglers' express'. It
was so named as each day it was always crowded with
passengers smuggling dairy products, alcohol and cigarettes
across the border. These items were still in short supply in
Northern Ireland but were much cheaper and readily available

in the Irish Republic. The return train leaving Belfast at 6 p.m. would be crowded with the same 'smugglers' this time wearing three dresses and four overcoats all newly bought. Clothes in Dublin were considered shoddy and the variety limited. Most passengers would be literally sweating when the Custom Men boarded the train at the border. This was not only from wearing all the extra clothes but also out of fear of having them confiscated.

Una finally received the longed for phone call from her cousin in Bangor. 'Forever Amber' was being shown the following week. We had all carefully been saving our pocket money for the fares.

On the appointed day we furtively boarded the train, our faces etched with guilt and fear. Once the train pulled out of Amiens Street Station and gathered speed we quickly relaxed and were soon devouring our sandwiches and chatting excitedly about our adventure. Our excitement was reaching boiling point when, just after midday, the train slid into Belfast Central. We lost no time in stopping a passer-by to ask directions to the nearest cinema showing our film. We were told 'The Regal' was no more then five minutes' walk away and found it easily. Then came our first disappointment.

'Look!' cried Mary; 'the cinema doesn't open until 3 o'clock.'
'Let's look for another one,' suggested Kate.
'Well it better not be far from the station or we'll never be back in time for the 6 o'clock train,' I reminded them. 'I think we'd better settle for this one, it's the nearest.' It was only 1 o'clock so we decided to have a look around the shops.
'This is awful,' murmured Bridget, 'all these lovely clothes and we can't afford so much as a pair of stockings.'
'Let's go into one of the bookshops and see what they have to

offer,' I ventured eagerly.
'Yeah!' was the instant reply.

We found one close to the cinema. An hour and a half later the shopkeeper was pleased to see us leave having leafed through most of his stock and giggled over the sexy bits that we'd read to one another in whispers.

'It's terrible we haven't any money, we could have made our fortune selling those books back home,' Una moaned on our way back to the cinema.

'That'd be dishonest,' I replied sanctimoniously, ignoring our own dishonesty just by being in Belfast.

As we entered the cinema we had our second shock.

'Look!' I whispered pointing to a notice by the ticket desk which read 'no one under the age of eighteen admitted' 'What are we going to do?'

'Let's go to the toilet for a start,' suggested Kate.

We all trundled into the toilet and immediately Kate produced a make-up purse from her bag and started to transform her face. She was the tallest and by far the most well-developed of us all. 'I'll get you in,' she bragged, 'I'm always taken for eighteen when I wear make-up.' We were all too much afraid of upsetting her by asking when she got the opportunity to wear make-up. We left the toilet and hid behind some posters advertising forthcoming attractions while she sashayed up to the ticket desk.

'Six ninepennies please'. Her voice squeaked but we needn't have worried, the bored girl behind the desk couldn't have cared less if we had been a band of headless wonders.

We sat in the darkened cinema with burning cheeks as the story unfolded; our hearts beating with an excitement slightly tinged by guilt, as we watched a BANNED film.

When the lights went up at the end, we walked from the cinema where shock number three awaited us. Who should be in front of us but Mrs. Reilly, our next door neighbour, and MY MOTHER! She turned around and winked at me.

'Not a word to your father. But it's a shame I didn't know you were coming, we could have bought a load more clothes that you and your friends could have worn across the border for us.' She said with a twinkle in her eye.

'Oh ma, you're terrible,' I blurted out.

'And so are you, lying about your picnic.' Then seeing our red faces she added kindly. 'Wasn't it great? Are you still in love with Cornel Wilde?'

'Yeah,' I smiled remembering I had a unique mother well ahead of her time.

'Listen you lot,' she continued, 'don't worry, I won't betray you, your secret is safe with me. I'll not mention it to anyone but make sure your picnics are no further than County Dublin for the rest of the holidays. Promise.'

'We promise,' we all echoed. We walked together to the station but being a thoughtful lady my mother made sure she and Mrs. Reilly sat well away from us. The journey back was pure magic, when we weren't discussing the film we were all agreeing I had a wonderful mother. This was no new discovery to me I always knew she was one in a million.

THE RELUCTANT FORTUNE-TELLER

Carol couldn't believe she had been so stupid to as let herself be persuaded. Her friends were right - she needed a good course in assertiveness training. Well, it was too late now to get out of this fix. She was on her way, on the hottest day in August, to the garden party at the local cancer hospice where she was to tell fortunes.

It was entirely Kevin's fault. Her brother had seemed strangely ill at ease when he came to dinner last week. He was sitting at the dining-room table making heavy weather of opening a bottle of wine while she was in the kitchen preparing their meal.
'You know how good you are at telling fortunes?' he shouted through the open door, à propos of nothing.
'What? Don't tell me you want your cards read? You know I don't do family,' she shouted back.
'No, of course not, but you know everyone says you have the gift.'
Carol began to feel apprehensive.
'Oh, I hate doing it, it takes too much out of me. I get very upset if I see anything bad.'

Carol arrived with the food and sat next to her brother, wondering what he was hinting at. Suddenly Kevin blurted out: 'At the Garden Party Committee Meeting the other night Jim was saying that we didn't make much of a profit for the charity last year and what we needed was some kind of gimmick. I suddenly remembered your gift at fortune telling and they jumped at the idea. I sort of promised I would get you to do it.' He had the grace to blush.
'How could you! I swore I'd never do it again after I saw Pat's death in the crystal. Anyway, it doesn't feel like a 'gimmick' to

me. I seem to be able to see into the future, that's why it upsets me so much.' Carol hesitated. She could see his embarrassment but she was still mad at him. 'You know I've never done it professionally, only for friends and then only one or two at a time,' she finished angrily.

'Well, just make it up, don't try to see their future. People only want to hear good news so you can tell them that they will live happily ever after, and we'll be happy with the money you'll make for the hospice.'

He had managed to hit on her Achilles heel - the hospice. Since visiting her friend Wendy there she had been impressed by the devotion shown by the hospice staff to all the patients. She continued to argue feebly but it was useless, she eventually gave in. Kevin left in high spirits - he wouldn't lose face in front of the committee.

'Don't worry, you might even enjoy it and they have got you a lovely blue tent,' he said cheerfully as he almost danced down the front steps.

Tent! Oh no, not a tent, in the middle of August. She went back inside and sank down on the couch. She felt like weeping and prayed for a dull, cool, wet day but immediately felt guilty, as that would mean no garden party and no money for the hospice.

She needn't have worried, her prayers weren't answered. The sun blazed high in the heavens. When she arrived at the hospice gate, Kevin was hovering anxiously and rushed up to her.

'Hurry up Carol, there's a queue formed already.' He ushered her towards the blue tent and to her horror she saw a large painted sign above the entrance 'Madame Astra, consultant to the stars of stage, screen and T.V.' Seeing the look on Carol's face Kevin tried to reassure her.

'We've placed the tent in the shade so it shouldn't get too hot,' he mumbled as he almost pushed her inside.

'OK, OK. But get me some ice cold water to keep me going. And I'm only doing it for two hours and not a minute longer,' she said positively.

'Of course, dear, anything you say, love,' he replied scurrying off to fulfil her request.

Soon she got into the swing, it was easy enough to tell the school children that they would pass all their exams and have a brilliant future. The teenagers were happy to hear that Mr. Right was just around the corner and she could judge by the faces of the older women whether their families had been a source of joy or sorrow. But it was still extremely tiring. The sun had followed its usual path and towards the end of her two hours it was shining directly onto the tent. Her hair was wet with perspiration and the ice cold water had become tepid. She glanced at her watch and realised she had done her stint. As she gathered her belongings, Jim, the Charity Chairman came in.

'That was great, everyone is singing your praises. I'll let you know how much we made in due course. Er ... I have a great favour to ask you?' he smiled trying to gauge her reaction. She continued to busy herself so he ventured on. 'The wife of one of our members is anxious to have her fortune told but she was delayed and has only just arrived. Do you think you could just squeeze in one more?' he pleaded. He looked so earnest that Carol took pity on him.

'OK, but this is definitely the last one,' she sighed.

Jim beat a hasty retreat and within minutes a small, sad-looking woman in her early sixties entered the tent. She was closely followed by a good-looking, fair-haired, well-built young man. Carol was annoyed, as she had stressed that only one person could enter at a time. She remained silent as she felt too tired to argue and the man seemed content to remain quietly just inside the entrance. She gave her usual spiel asking the woman if she wanted her cards read or the crystal. The woman answered in a low voice asking for the crystal.

Once Carol started she suddenly realised that she was actually reading the crystal and could not fob off this person with a pack of lies. She was overwhelmed by the sorrow emanating from the woman.
'I wish I could tell you everything is going to be alright but all I can see is darkness surrounding you. I see a man in bed, he looks very old and frail and is in a lot of pain.' The woman interrupted her.
'He's not that old,' the woman told her, 'he's only sixty-two.'
She started to sob quietly. The young man came up and put his hand gently on her shoulder.
'Don't worry, I will never leave you. I'll always be there whenever you need me,' he said soothingly.
The woman didn't seem to hear but stood up and walked wearily from the tent followed by the young man.
Carol sat alone feeling incredibly sad. It was some minutes before she could force herself into the sunlight. Emerging she saw Jim with his arms around the woman walking her towards his car. The young man was nowhere to be seen.

Kevin came running up to her.
'Oh thanks, sis. My God you look as if you need a drink. Come on I'll treat you,' he said guiding her towards the bar. He seated her at a table by the window and went to buy the drinks. 'I see Jim got you to tell Mrs. Brennan's fortune. I think she was hoping you'd tell her Jack would recover. He's a patient here in the hospice,' Kevin commented as he placed the drinks on the table.

Carol shook her head sadly and was very grateful for the large gin and tonic before returning to her flat. Next morning Kevin phoned her.

'You'll be glad to know we made £350 on the fortune telling,' he announced. 'What about doing it again next year?'

'You must be joking, that was the last time I tell fortunes. I can't bear the pain I see,' she cried.

'I know, I'm sorry. By the way, Jack Brennan died last night.'

'Oh no. I saw it was imminent. Thank God she has such a lovely son to look after her,' Carol commented.

'What are you on about. She has no son, they never had any children,' Kevin retorted.

'But who was the young man that came into the tent with her?' she asked.

'The sun must have got to you - no one went into the tent with her, I was right outside, she was on her own,' he replied.

'Kevin, did you know them well?' she asked hesitantly.

'Oh, yes, for about thirty-five years.'

'What was he like when he was young?'

'He was tall, fair haired, a well-built good looking man.

It was terrible what the cancer did to his body.'

Carol put the phone back in its cradle, feeling weak and dizzy. That was it. The certain discovery that she had indeed the ability to see into the future terrified her. Never, ever again would she as much read a tea cup, but she made a vow to herself that, when the time was right, she would get Mrs. Brennan's address and visit her. She would tell her how she knew that Jack would always be close by, protecting and looking after her.

Tui Alba

New Zealand born Tui Alba, worked for newspapers, radio and TV in her homeland before coming to Europe in the early sixties. She wanted to do things, not write about them.

An accomplished dancer Tui worked in cabaret in England and Western Europe. When resting she worked as a chambermaid and claims she can make a bed in any language.

Now settled in England Tui has had many enterprising jobs (shoe-shining to name one) but her quest for enlightenment has made her something of an eternal student. She has a Counselling Certificate and a Diploma in Applied Psychology, both with distinction and hard-earned from Birkbeck.

With the encouragement of her Cockney husband Ted and the patience of her cats Troubles and Treasures, Tui re-launched her writing career. Writing as Tui Grimmer-Fleming she contributed two chapters to counseling and Older People published by Age Concern.Tui campaigns for Action on Elder Abuse and is a mediator with CALM (Confidential and Local Mediation Service), which intercedes in neighbour disputes.

THE WALKMAN

He was one of 'them' - definitely one of 'them' - she decided, venting her resentment on the umbrella she was carrying, banging it open against the heavy shopping trolley.

'Why is my life plagued with 'them'? Sue thought out loud as she struggled along dragging the trolley with one hand and holding her umbrella in front of her like a riot shield against the driving rain. 'Now they've even got me talking to myself, the bloody jobsworths,' she blurted out, her voice rising to compete with the gusting wind.

'Why is life always them and us? They control every bloody thing. They let us think we've got rights and when we try to exercise them we discover that we haven't got any at all. Bloody receipt the man wanted. The shop's name was on the bloody Walkman, it couldn't have been bought anywhere else. How did I keep a civil tongue in my head? I did ask him ever so politely, How could I have a bloody receipt? It was a present.'

'Shit,' Sue fumed at the wet pavement. 'I'm too damn soft for my own good,' she tormented herself, 'they always walk over me, I should have stood my ground, I shouldn't have been so reasonable and understood that it was shop policy that they had to have a receipt. Or proof of purchase the man had said. How the hell did I keep my temper when I told him yet again that it was a present and there was no way I could lay my hands on a receipt.'

A squall of wind whipped the umbrella inside out, and Sue swore colourfully and seriously as she struggled to right it, getting miserably wet at the same time. 'All that niceness didn't get my damn Walkman fixed, did it? And they've got me bloody swearing again.'

Sue let herself into the flat, stood the dripping umbrella in the sink and glared at the trolley now making dirty puddles on her clean floor. She sighed as she regarded her rain-flattened prized puffer jacket and bemoaned her fading tan as she toweled off her bare legs. She then unpacked her shopping, plugged the kettle in and snapped on the telly. It came quickly to life extolling the virtues of the high street electrical chain that had just given her so much aggro. 'We always put our customers first,' some rap band chanted. 'You bloody liars, no you bloody don't,' she screamed futilely at the TV.

Sue continued to swear and curse herself hoarse while she kicked the shopping trolley ail over the room, punishing it as if it was one of 'them'. It was the only way she could stop herself from smashing up one of their products, the mocking television set.

...ooOoo...

Alan watched the little Essex stereotype bustle out of the shop, her high heels clicking in an exacerbated manner, betraying her aggravation. Her frustration matched his own. 'You're the youngest in the district,' his Area Supervisor had told him when he had given him his Manager's badge. 'This shop's yours now, look after it well and in ten years time you could be on the Board,' the man who looked like a sleazy sales rep had said in what passed for a joking manner.

'Seriously though,' he had added, 'keep the paperwork in order and the slippage down and you'll do OK.' Well, he had kept the paperwork in order and his slippage, the store's jargon for shoplifting, was better than most. His worst incident had been last week when he had had to deal with a particularly nasty skinhead who was trying to pass off a bent credit card. He had kept the card but lost the goods. He reported the matter to the police, he had to for his records, but knew the chances of catching the sod were pretty remote. The pictures off the closed circuit security cameras were worse than useless, head office couldn't spend money on clarity tapes. The cameras were the deterrent, he was told. 'I wish they'd get real,' he thought dejectedly.

What his Area hadn't said, nor had any of his training given much instruction on, was how much time and effort he would have to put into dealing with customers' complaints. Each week he parcelled up several boxes of goods that had been returned as faulty and sent them back to the depot.

The trouble was that most of the electronic stuff was a poor rip-off of the branded master, but he couldn't tell the customers that of course. The store advertised its own label as value far money, and most customers were penny wise and pound foolish. 'They think buying electronics is the same as buying baked beans,' Area had said by way of patronising understanding.

The day had started out badly. There had been a storm overnight and as always the lightning had played havoc with the atmospherics, triggering all the circuit breakers, and he had spent most of the morning getting the computerised tills and stack controls back online.

And now here was yet another dissatisfied customer thrusting another of the shop's 'doesn't work' goods at him. Alan listened resignedly to the customer and told her with much practiced calm that he couldn't do anything without proof of purchase. He couldn't very well tell her that he had heard variations of the present story at least a hundred times before and he could take odds-on bets that the Walkman she held in her hand had been stolen.

He invited her over to the counter where he could check stack records and the store's gift file and see if it had been recorded there. She stood obligingly in front of the secret camera that took mug shots of suspected frauds. She seemed genuine enough though when she kept insisting that she neither wanted to exchange the Walkman for anything else nor wanted money back, she just wanted her present fixed.

Alan handed the personal stereo back to her, saying that he really was sorry but there was nothing he could do - store policy and all that - he had to have a receipt.

...ooOoo...

'What' s all this?' Wayne' s voice cut through Sue's misery. His stockiness and swagger commanded her attention. 'What's 'appened to the trolley?'

Sue explained all about the shop and its bloody policy, carefully ignoring the trolley's fate. He would never understand how being a person with rights was so important to her, and he would never understand the value she put on presents.
'You stupid cow,' Wayne reacted, 'why didn't ya tell me it was bust before ya went barging off and making waves?' He saw her alarmed look, he saw the question marks forming in her eyes. 'Don't worry about it, I'll see me man and get you another.'
To head off any further protest Wayne stuck his hand in his pocket and pulled out a twenty pound note. 'Helped ol' Joe move some furniture,' he said by way of explanation. 'It's stopped raining, why don't ya nip down the offy and get us one of them wine boxes? An' while ya there get an appointment for your roots!'
'I'm growing it out, I'm fed up with blonde,' Sue said with a finality in her voice that told Wayne to quit while he was ahead.

She took the money and pulled on her still damp puffer. She could have argued that the money would be better spent on the gas bill but didn't have the energy.

…ooOoo…

Alan saw 'Essex' as he climbed down the ladder. He had just replaced the fluorescent tube in the store's fascia - another casualty of last night's storm. He put his screwdriver in his pocket and fingered the mug shot he had taken earlier of her. There was something about her, something that had made him trouser the photo rather than follow procedure and include it in the internal mail.

'Whatever happened to the trolley?' he asked. As chat-up lines go it was pretty good for a dull Monday afternoon.

'The wind,' Sue answered lamely, surprised at herself for even recognising, let alone speaking to, this representative of 'them'. Especially when he was solely responsible for this trolley's battering.

Alan checked her wedding finger. It was ring-less. That didn't mean she was unattached but perhaps he was in with a chance. He exercised his sales training, put on his professional smile, and pressed his advantage. 'I'm pleased I saw you, we've had a new circular come on since I saw you this morning. That model of Walkman has been recalled. It's got a fault that can't be repaired, but I can replace it.'

'Oh!' Sue muttered, fed up with the whole business. Perhaps she had got him wrong; perhaps he wasn't so bloody bad after all. She gave him the once-over. He was presentable in a straight sort of way. He was taller and slimmer than Wayne and he had hair. A curly brown head of it.

'I' m off tomorrow, bring it in Wednesday. Make sure you ask for me, Alan.' Fiddling the necessary paperwork would be simple, getting her to go out with him, now that might prove more tricky.

...ooOoo...

Sue stretched and felt the nausea of the hangover hit her. She must have passed out. 'Well what did he bloody expect? All that booze on an empty stomach and at five in the afternoon,' Sue went into automatic excuse mode. She couldn't remember whether she had staggered onto this kitchen couch or whether Wayne had carried her there. 'He probably screwed me too' Sue speculated, cursing the blackout, as she stood up adjusting her knickers and straightening her mini-skirt. 'I hope I enjoyed it.' 'Oh hell, look at the time, it's gone bloody midnight.' Sue could hear the words, could feel the black mood; 'Bloody anti-social bitch,' and 'I see more of the cat than I do of you,' followed by 'that's the last time I buy you a drink.' She'd better clean her teeth, take a couple of aspirins and a long gulp of water before she faced him.

Sue took a deep breath, 'Oh stuff him,' she snarled at the bathroom mirror, 'I don't have to take his crap.' Even looking this rough she was still fanciable; that 'them' had given her the come-on. The remnants of the alcohol were making her argumentative.

She squared her shoulders and defensively opened the living room door. Wayne wasn't there. Gone to bed with the sulks, she supposed. Oh well, she' d have a hot chocolate and a fag and turn in, his silence was better than a row and at least she'd get some sleep. A stiff back was better than a night of restless, 'I can't sleep with all your nagging.'

It was almost one o'clock and if she was going to go to bed she'd better go now. She quietly opened the bedroom door to fetch her baggy sleeping T-shirt. He wasn't there either. Sue was baffled. Where the hell was he? What was going on? She hadn't any idea why she did it, but she searched the flat again. She even called his name, louder each time.

If he was out getting a skin-full with his mates ... she'd! Well she wasn't quite sure what she would do.

…ooOoo…

Another hour passed and with it her hangover. Sue reasoned that since Wayne's car had the raunchiest engine in the street she'd at least have enough warning to greet him with loving concern, then she realised that the car keys were on their hook, but maybe he was using a spare set.

Oblivious to the fact that it was drizzling again, Sue went out and scanned the street. Ah there it was, in his least favourite place, parked under a tree. Ideal, Wayne claimed, for collecting paint-damaging bird-shit.

'You're out late,' Alan panted as he recognised 'Essex.' He marked time beside her; he liked to jog in the early hours. 'Live near here? Had a nice evening?'

'What's with all the questions?' Sue snarled, started. What the hell was 'them' doing here?

'See you tomorrow.'

'Yeah,' Sue said as she scuttled inside. She passed the bruised trolley on the way in and resisted the urge to give it another savage kick. She would have to get a grip on herself till she found out where Wayne had been and what he had been up to. He'd find out soon enough that he couldn't play head games with her. He'd pay for his night's sport.

The shrill scream of the doorbell cut through her vengeful thoughts. What the hell was it at this hour? If he's lost his keys well he can bloody well go back where he was. 'Who is it?' Sue shrieked through the door.

'Police, Madam, open up!'

'Police?'

'Open the door, we have a warrant!'

Sue squinted through the spy hole. It was indeed the Old Bill. She opened the door, horror replacing anger. A battered, sheepish Wayne trailed in behind them.

'What's this all about? How did you get bloody?' Sue demanded.

'It weren't nothin',' Wayne blustered, 'just a misunderstandin' in the pub. They' re just making a busy of themselves. Told 'em there ain' t nothin' here.'

The 'them,' with stripes had picked up her Walkman off the coffee table as he walked in. He turned it over in his hand. 'Got you mister, regular film star you are!' he stated, pulling out of his pocket a photocopy of a still from a shop's closed circuit video tape depicting a fuzzy but recognisable Wayne hoisting the little radio. 'Definitely copped in action a week ago wasn't he constable! Anything else here?' he continued menacingly at Wayne, brandishing her Walkman triumphantly under his nose.

'Na, I swear there's not and that's hers,' Wayne whined.

'Is this the only one here?' the sergeant asked pointing this offending object at Sue.

'Yes, and he gave it to me.'

The sergeant's eyes swept the room. It was dole furniture and benefit fittings. Experience told him that if he wanted he could probably find more questionable items, but the radio was enough for a result.

'Want me to give it the once over, Sarge?' the constable checked, looking eager to search the flat.

'Do that!' Stripes now scanned Sue; in her favour was that she was clean and she kept the place tidy and he wasn't into arresting wives if he could avoid it. 'You're sure he got it and he gave it to you?'

'Yes, yes.'

'I'll believe you this once,' stripes said, looking threateningly at Sue. The constable came back into the room. He shook his head.

'There' s nothing Sarge.'

'Come on you, let's get you charged,' the big policeman said firmly, ordering Wayne to the panda car.

'What happens now?' Sue ventured, recovering her senses. The whole thing seemed virtual; it felt like being in a bad TV drama.

'He'll be charged with handling stolen goods and bailed to appear in court in the morning,' the constable told her.

Sue watched the panda disappear down the street; it was almost daylight. She lit a fag, and headed for bed, there was nothing else she could do.

…ooOoo…

Sue had heard Wayne come home around six and then spent what was left of the night watching the satellite sport channel. He wasn't game enough to come to bed and explain. She had been brooding on the events of yesterday and last night. One unanswered question had chased another through her head and each miserable thought had fuelled another bitter resentment. How dare he give her stolen goods and say they were a present. And her making a fool of herself in the store over that precious gift, and getting her drunk on bent money, and all the other. But most of all, if he was spending his time out thieving why hadn't he told her, at least she could have walked away. She had her pride.

She trudged into the kitchen and began to get breakfast. Wayne slammed the front door, he had been to get the newspaper.
He ignored her, he had nothing to say to her, she'd put him right in it. Well if that's his game, Sue thought, I can do silence too. Wayne rustled the paper and thrust his elbows out across the table, holding the tabloid at its fullest extent, reducing the usable part of the small kitchen bar to the size of a tea tray.

Sue deliberately picked up her toast knife and stabbed it through the paper, rending a sizable hole which framed a filthy look. Wayne made a growling sound through his teeth and deliberately folded the paper in half, letting the page's edges sag down into her coffee. Sue picked up her ruined coffee, leaned over the paper barricade and poured it into Wayne's glass. She watched fascinated as the coffee curdled the orange juice into a frothy foul brew.

Wayne's knuckles went white with suppressed fury. Today of all days, what with him due in court in two hours, couldn't she at least let him have breakfast in peace. He picked up the foul brew and with a look of menace poured it over her uneaten cornflakes.

Sue's arm was stopped in full swing as Wayne stood up preventing her from throwing the plate of soggy cereal. Without letting go of her arm, he swung it behind her back and propelled her out of the kitchen door into the garden, locking the door behind her.

Cuddling herself tight to hold in her tears of misery Sue shivered in the dampness. She was about to bang on the door and say sorry when she saw Wayne open the fridge and pick out a beer. He flicked the ring-pull in her direction and grunted in satisfaction as it hit the window, then he turned his back and sat down to read the sport pages. Her self-pity dissolved into contempt 'Right! That's bloody it! I'm out of here, you've just blown any damn chance of help from me.'

...ooOoo...

Alan had spied as the cops came and went last night. He had keenly observed the drama played out in the curtainless kitchen next door. Determinedly he opened his back door and walked out into the garden. 'Don't get involved, it's none of your business,' common sense told him. But Alan was being led by his loins and his 'Essex' was in trouble.
'Come on,' he urged as he held out his arms to help her over the dividing wall. 'I've got a punch bag you can play with.'
Sue peered at him for a long decisive moment. She had been so betrayed by 'us' it was time to discover 'them.'

Val Creegan

Val was born in Germany. She has lived in Geneva, Paris and Dublin and is now living in London with her husband. She has two daughters. She has written a novel in German and is now writing in English.

HANS DÖBLIN LEAVES SUDDENLY

Hans Döblin decided overnight that he had to disappear. In his mid-forties, grey-eyed, ash-blond, but greying at the temples, he still had the figure of an athlete and was a handsome man.

A neighbour had told Hans that he had had enough of the 'goings-on' and was going to denounce him to the Board of Governors of the school where Hans taught literature. Suddenly Hans found himself in a position that was socially unacceptable to some of his colleagues and for some reason he felt morally somewhat shabby.

Hans decided to leave for California. He did not overtly encourage Edgar to go with him, but he came anyway. 'I'm bored in this bloody small town, bored out of my brain,' he said. 'It's time I had a change.' Hans was thrilled; this then was a joint decision.

For a time they managed in Los Angeles, Hans as a replacement teacher, Edgar working in a hairdressing salon.

Edgar was dark-blond, green-eyed with an alabaster skin and an elegant physique. He was intelligent, but not well educated. Edgar did not express himself in a sophisticated way, but Hans never spoke to him with the authoritative voice of a teacher to his pupil, because he loved him. Hans was gentle and kind because that was his nature. He knew that Edgar had never felt safe at home, not as long as his father had been alive, for he had detested the boy and his effeminate ways. Hans wanted to protect and cherish Edgar. He believed that after childhood, when we accept anything, we wake up one day to reality and the precariousness of existence. Edgar had escaped from home by joining the boys' choir and assisting at Mass, but of course this stopped when he grew older. Edgar was not interested in reading unlike Hans who, by the time he was a teenager, had already read every book in the library of the small town where he grew up and had to bike to the nearest town for further material.

Edgar had a fine body, elegant, slender hands and he moved with such grace that just looking at him filled Hans with joy. No matter how much Edgar ate his stomach remained flat and he never put on weight. He smoked and drank, but nothing could diminish his beauty. It was, of course, due to his incredible youth, Hans thought with a pang, for Edgar was almost 20 years younger than he was.

To have Edgar living with him was a constant source of delight. It gave Hans a feeling of belonging, something he had never known before. He also felt responsible for Edgar's wellbeing.

When Edgar came home, Hans felt a sense of perfect joy rush through his body making him dizzy. When Edgar's profile turned towards him it moved him unbearably and at the same time made him fiercely protective - all vanities, all ambitions were gone.

Edgar's light-hearted behaviour delighted Hans. His angelic smile, his lack of reserve, the urgency of his whispers made Hans shiver with delight. When Hans held him in his arms, he felt complete, his love was unconditional and could not be measured. The sky was full of celebrating stars.

When Edgar was late home, Hans sometimes wondered whether he was generous elsewhere with his sexual favours - but then dismissed the thought as unworthy. However, he became aware of the fragility of their relationship, that his love made him vulnerable, and he felt unaccountably lonely.

'I met this guy in a pub,' Edgar said to Hans one evening - there was a scent of excitement in his voice when he spoke - 'he gave me this address in Hollywood. I'm bored in my job, I want to get away.' 'Yes,' Hans said,"I can see that.' He walked across the room, moving on automatic pilot. He was not included.

Edgar smiled and the thought occurred to Hans how heartless his light-hearted gaiety really was. He felt a moment of envy, almost of hatred, then dismissed the feeling, but found he was sweating profusely. In a last attempt Hans reached out to Edgar. He felt that the power of his affection would surely hold him back, but Edgar turned away. Hans had the sensation of being sucked down into a quagmire.

So that was it, that was what rejection felt like. He should have expected it, Edgar was so young and eager to live. 'When is it to be?' Hans asked when he found his voice. 'Tomorrow,' Edgar replied curtly, 'I'm going to pack.' In long strides he went upstairs to their bedroom, where Hans had hung up his ironed shirts and neatly folded his underwear and socks to keep disorder at bay.

'Do you mind if I take yours?' Edgar asked leaning over the banister and holding up Hans' favourite suitcase. Hans nodded in assent.

We are minor players in a melodrama, with only God watching and He doesn't care, he thought brokenly.

The next day Hans kissed Edgar on the forehead. 'God's speed, I wish you well!' he said as Edgar went. The door shut behind him. Hans was overcome by grief: what sort of life would he have all on his own without Edgar?

Hans was unable to sleep. He took sugared tea with a few slugs of whisky before going to bed, but it did not help and eventually he had to resort to sleeping pills. When he woke up he was still monstrously tired and deeply depressed. His days seemed burdensome and endless; anxiety and anger extended into weeks. Hans felt that he was finally going to pieces. 'Dear God,' he found himself praying, 'help me!'

'I should be pleased because I am alive and halfway sane,' Hans thought. 'Pull yourself together!' he addressed himself. 'Find your own Kingdom of Heaven!' He inhaled and exhaled slowly and deeply and closed his eyes. He imagined that he was sitting in a white light. He was sitting for quite a while, breathing slowly and deeply and he felt a stillness in the room. Suddenly he felt his despair lifting.

Hans smiled into the mirror and stood there thinking for while. Then he packed an overnight bag and went for the weekend to San Francisco. When the mist lifted, Hans saw the light blue sky, the azure pools dotted between shell-pink houses, the palm trees, the parrots with kingfisher-blue, sienna, charcoal, lemon and apple-green feathers and wondered what they ate to keep up their incredible plumage. He saw red admirals, light green butterflies and bright blue birds. The air was wild with the scent of herbs and flowers.

The heavenly aroma of freshly roasted coffee wafting through the open door of a cafe made Hans enter and order breakfast, complete with blueberry muffins and pancakes with maple syrup. The leisurely pace and easy-going charm of the people made him feel welcome. It was a homecoming after a long and tiring journey. He looked at the world once again with a kindly eye.

Hans went back to Los Angeles to fetch his belongings. He then set about finding an apartment to rent. By word of mouth he found himself a job, teaching literature.

Hans was suddenly assailed by uncertainty: did he have anything valuable to say to his students? He had to face his own insecurities and self-hate. He had to face his demons and find the answer in his own heart. 'It is true that when we begin a new life,' he thought, 'resistance flies in our face.' 'Don't be tossed on the rubbish-heap, but look at your obsessions, your anxious thoughts, write them down and see how silly they are. If I'm not afraid of my own voice,' Hans said to himself, 'if I have a safe place in my own heart, I will not fear the world.'

Hans had wanted to be a teacher for as long as he could remember, to instil the love of literature in young people, to teach them to make a choice for clear truth and beauty, to do their work as well as they could, and be kind. This, he thought, would be his contribution to making the world a better place. If every person did his or her best then it would become better. It was that simple. Hans' students sat in a circle on the green carpet. Through the rectangle of the window he could see the indigo blue sky. It was a happy day.

Over time Hans got to know and love his students. He gave them permission to think and to make sense of their thoughts in any way they wished, a lesson in self-discovery. 'Young people are bright,' Hans thought, 'they write down their thoughts to inform themselves.'

San Francisco was enchanting. Hans looked at the light blue Californian sky, the display of giant cacti and bright flowers, the tiny scarlet birds, the large lizards sunning themselves on a rock and thought himself lucky.

He swam 20 lengths of the pool every morning and went to yoga classes to learn about relaxation and meditation. 'Breathe out your fears and worries,' the teacher said, 'and breathe in faith in the future, hope and love and concentrate on the life-giving, joy-giving, peace-giving force.'

When Edgar had left, Hans had thought that life was over, that he would not be able to function without him. But he found that he could function very well and indeed make a new beginning.

What he needed now was the briskness and intelligence of his peers. Hans set about meeting his colleagues once or twice a week. He could learn a lot from them and was grateful for their tolerance and companionship.

One Sunday he went up the hill to the little whitewashed church. The preacher told the congregation of the redemptive power of prayer and hope. 'How blessed are those who know their need of God,' he said. He told them of God's loving-kindness. 'He looks on us favourably and what flows from that is security and a feeling of well-being. God is love,' the preacher said. 'To live by grace is to be transformed.' From that day on Hans went to church regularly.

He had known the ecstasy of shivering delight, but that was behind him.
'Are you lonely?' he asked himself. Did he need more than undemanding friendship? Did he need solace in the form of sexual favours? Hans could answer that at the moment he was fine and would let things quietly work themselves out.

If he were to sit down and make a list of everything that he wanted from life, it would not be so very much. How one changed! The shock of Edgar leaving (he had written a postcard from Hollywood saying that he had been engaged by a filmstar as his personal hairdresser) had been a great help to set him on the road to self-discovery. A journey towards grace and forgiveness had begun.

THE PARTNER

It was a weekend in May. Maria carried a tall vase filled with delphiniums and put it down on the polished refectory table with its sturdy crossbar and solid legs. She stood back to admire them; the mild blue colour was enchanting. There was a painting on the wall, an abstract, in aubergine, pale lemon, light green and milk-white. On the bookshelves were the tans and reds of leather-bound volumes of her book collection - some first editions. It was quiet in the room with its floor length windows. There was almost an air of serenity.

Maria looked out of the window. A red Porsche purred by followed by a dark-blue Mercedes. The house opposite had scarlet geraniums in terracotta pots on the sills. The trees in the garden swayed elegantly, they were still decked out in light. A few people hastened by and a little dog was running back and forth, barking with a great deal of anger. Then she saw Charles in a pink shirt and pinstriped suit walking on the other side, stiff-backed like a gander. 'Do people remark about the way I walk?' he asked Peter, her husband, who met him now and then for a drink. 'Have you a bad back?' he asked. 'It is actually MS,' Charles replied. 'I could end up in a wheelchair - unless they find a cure soon.' Charles walked on, moving his furled umbrella up and down. Suddenly Maria glimpsed Joy across the road: silver-haired, statuesque. She was her ex-neighbour who would pop around the back and bring her an armful of spinach or a few tomatoes straight out of the garden, still smelling of sun and air. When she turned around, it wasn't her.

Peter came home and bent down to kiss her. He brought his partner Jean-Paul with him. Peter was an architect. He was tall and had the physique of a sportsman. He had dark-blond hair, a broad, good-humoured face, blue eyes and a high forehead. Peter was intelligent; he was popular, because he was always smiling, gallant and obliging. If someone's life were blighted, he would do what he could to help. Peter assumed that all people were like him: honest, helpful and full of goodwill towards mankind. Maria had the feeling that she had to protect him to stop him from being exploited.

Jean-Paul was a thirty year old Frenchman with curly blond hair, small grey-green eyes and strong glasses. They had met during their studies. Peter gave Jean-Paul his full confidence. Jean-Paul was a born raconteur and with his charming accent he proceeded to tell one anecdote after another. Peter slapped his thighs and laughed merrily. They had not long ago moved to London and were glad to have such a nice friend.

Peter had invited Jean-Paul for drinks and he had brought a bottle of wine and a spectacular box of chocolates. 'My oh my,' said Peter in an American accent, 'will you look at these, girl!' Jean-Paul was brought up by his grandmother, as there were five children and not enough room at home. 'Didn't you miss your parents and brothers and sisters?' Maria asked when he told her about it. 'Not at all, grandmère spoilt me rotten,' replied Jean-Paul. He had no family in England and visited them often. 'On Saturday, I usually cook myself a large casserole,' he told them, 'it would last me quite a few days, but the people I share the house with help themselves and when I get home the pot is empty. From now on I am going to put the casserole into the boot of my car to keep it safe.' Maria had to laugh. 'I wouldn't do it when it gets warmer. You can come to us as often as you like.' 'You are very generous hosts,' said Jean-Paul and combed his blond curls with his fingers.

Peter went out to get more wine. Maria went into the kitchen to make some sandwiches, ham and cheese on rye bread. 'Maria, vous etes une belle femme,' said Jean-Paul. 'Compliments are always welcome,' she replied. 'Have you never thought of getting married?' J'étais marié une fois,' answered Jean-Paul. 'Were you not happy?' 'I was barely twenty and in the middle of my studies. My family was against it…It was a mistake.' 'Mon pauvre!' 'Don't pity me,' answered Jean-Paul. ' I am a randy fellow and get easily bored. I like change.'

Peter returned and filled the glasses. They were merry and decided to go to a nightclub. When they got there, Peter saw one of their employees and asked her for a dance. 'Shall we?' said Jean-Paul. Maria was a little tipsy and took his arm. When they danced Jean-Paul held her too close. 'I find it difficult to breathe,' Maria said and freed herself. They made their way back to their table and ordered another round.

The waitress came and banged the bottle down on the table. She was beautiful like a model with long dark hair and large almond-shaped eyes. 'Is anything the matter?' enquired Peter. The waitress looked at Jean-Paul with contempt and took her leave. 'I had a rendezvous with her and completely forgot about it,' Jean-Paul shrugged ruefully with his shoulders. 'Barbara,' he addressed the waitress when she returned to collect the money, 'I am so terribly sorry.' 'Is that so?' He took her hand. 'Leave me alone, shithead!' 'Barbara, how about something to eat? We are starving!' he pleaded. 'Maybe some spare-ribs of pork - if there are any.' Barbara returned and put an oval platter of bones in front of Jean-Paul. 'Oh alors! I think I have offended her.' He pulled a funny face. His lips were thick and almost black from the red wine he had drank.

'Does it happen frequently that you forget a rendezvous?' asked Peter. 'Now and then,' admitted Jean-Paul. 'I go out with a girl once and by the end of the evening I am already fed up with her. Soon after I got married I was eyeing other girls until my wife had enough and threw me out. I am very fickle.' 'Yes you are,' laughed Peter, 'especially when you have drunk too much, then you will stop at nothing.' 'Once I was so soulé,' said Jean-Paul, 'and drove at such a high speed that a police-car was chasing me. I drove straight to an acquaintance and parked my car in his garage. Later I got rid of it and bought another one.'

A few days later Maria came home from work and was about to open the front door when someone put a hand on her shoulder. It was Inge, a friend from back home. 'What a surprise!' 'I would have phoned you,' she said, 'but I couldn't get hold of your phone number.' Inge had cool grey eyes, a thin straight nose, light brown hair done in a French pleat and a severe mouth. She wore a beautifully cut grey suit and had a formidable presence. When she took off her jacket, Maria saw that she still had her lovely, big-busted figure with the tiny waist. When she complimented her and told her that she had always admired her figure, Inge shrugged. 'You, Maria, have the legs; I, the bust. Together we would make the ideal woman.' They burst out laughing. Later on Peter brought Jean-Paul along and they had a few drinks together. At around midnight Jean-Paul saw Inge to her hotel.

Two days later Inge phoned. 'Can I come around?' 'Of course, do come!' 'I have decided to stay on for a bit,' she said when Maria answered the door. She offered Inge a glass of wine. "Tell me,' she said, 'have you known Jean-Paul for long?' 'Six months or so - why?' 'I like him, he is very self-confident and charming. We spent a few nice evenings together. Is he married?' 'Jean-Paul got married very young,' Maria replied. 'He is either divorced or separated, I am not sure which.' After a while Inge said: 'I must go, I have a rendezvous with Jean-Paul.'

Peter had to go away for a week on a business trip. Maria had just come home, she had had a hectic day and was tired. I will make myself an omelette and a green salad and then go to bed with a book, she thought and hummed to herself. Or maybe I'll do some writing - all one needs is a bit of passion!

The bell rang. It was Jean-Paul. 'Pour toi,' he said and put a bottle of champagne and a basket of strawberries on the table. He went into the kitchen and Maria looked out of the window. There was a disturbance outside where the wind was stirring the trees. The long branches were streaming in the wind.

Jean-Paul returned with glasses. 'Sit down!' he ordered and behaved as if at home. 'Relax e-toi!' He got up and sat closer to her. 'What shall I do with all these strawberries?' 'Watch!' Jean-Paul dipped a large juicy berry into the glass of champagne and popped it into her mouth. 'Maria, tu es trés belle,' he said. 'Je t'adore. I could fall in love with you.' 'What about Inge?'she teased him. 'Inge? Mon dieu, it is nothing serious. I was just nice to her because she is your friend. I only fall for women like you - reticent, mysterious.' 'Leave it, Jean-Paul!' said Maria who preferred her friends to show some decorum. 'You are our friend and Peter's partner.' ' I know,' he said ruefully, 'but you should enjoy life a little - like Peter,' Jean-Paul continued. 'I don't suppose you know that he takes his secretary to expensive restaurants for lunch.' 'I would have thought this common practice.' 'Well, last week Peter took her out three times.' 'I don't mind,' Maria replied, suddenly pensive. Peter's secretary was eighteen, blonde and very pretty. 'If I were married to you, I wouldn't leave you alone for a week,' said Jean-Paul. 'I am a passionate Frenchman: we Français enjoy making l'amour. We love les femmes - unlike the Englishmen who prefer young boys.' 'You don't really believe that?' 'I do. I suppose you have heard of 'le vice anglais' - that's what we call homosexuality.' 'You are unbelievable,' Maria said, 'but I am tired, you must go.' Reluctantly Jean-Paul got up and left. He's got a nerve! she thought and looked out of the window to see him climb into his car and drive away. The wind had died down. There was a hedge to one side of the garden and a sea of flowers, creamy white, pale pink, violet and deep purple.

Maria fell into bed, revelling in her childish glee for sleep.

Two days later Maria answered the door to Jean-Paul. He had tears in his eyes. 'Come in! What has happened?' 'Maman et grandmère died in a fire,' he sobbed and buried his face in his hands. 'Oh, my God!' she cried aghast. 'The house was burning so fiercely, les pompiers couldn't get close. It burned to the ground. I am flying home in the early hours.' Jean-Paul was in a terrible state, He was shivering as he sweated; he was overwhelmed by grief. His eyes were red-rimmed, he could barely speak and was shaking badly. Maria made him sit down and put her arms around him. 'You poor boy, I am so very sorry…How terrible!' She rocked him in her arms. Eventually she succeeded in calming Jean-Paul a bit and got up to make him a cup of hot, sweet tea.

'Tu es bonne,' said Jean-Paul; he took Maria's hand and kissed it. Then he knelt on the floor and to her consternation he started kissing her feet. Poor boy, she thought, he is distraught. She stroked his curly blond mop. 'Get up, Jean-Paul!' He encircled her knees and caressed her legs. When he started to sob again, Maria pulled him into her arms and held him. They started making love. When Jean-Paul left it was very late.

The next day, as Maria inserted the key into the front door, she could hear the phone ringing. It was Inge. 'Have you heard the terrible news?' Maria asked. 'What news?' 'Jean-Paul's mother and grandmother died in a fire. The house burnt down to the ground. He has gone over for the funeral.' 'What funeral?' Inge said. 'I have just seen Jean-Paul, he didn't mention anything.' Maria was longing to confide in her, but found that she couldn't talk about it. Slowly she put down the receiver. She went to the window and looked out. The light was dimming. The clouds were hanging low, a strange white light was behind them. A black cat was going about his business. She could see the leaves on the bushes tremble.

A chill spread downward through her stomach. Maria had been totally fooled by Jean-Paul, totally unaware of his intentions. She marvelled at her own innocence. This is a bad day, she thought and could hardly breathe for her sorrow. She lay down, turned her head from side to side and began to cry.

It was late in the evening. A blood-orange sun sank and disappeared into the horizon. The doorbell rang. Maria felt a touch of unease. She could see from the window that it was Jean-Paul who was standing outside. The air around her grew tight. A quick sigh escaped her. She missed Peter with his beneficent smile.

I won't go to the door, she thought, but Jean-Paul had his finger on the doorbell. 'If you don't open the door, I'll kick it in!' he shouted through the letterbox. 'Then you'll have to explain to Peter why.' She thought of Peter and her love for him. He was a good man. He paid everything she said the honour of his serious attention. Without him she felt very much alone. Maria felt a touch of fear and the violent beating of her heart. She was more vulnerable than she ever could have imagined.
Maria confronted Jean-Paul at the door, trying to keep the

agitation out of her voice. Fear had its special aroma. Could he smell it? 'You cannot come in!' 'He! He!' he cackled, 'is that so?' He watched her with sly amusement. 'Tell me,' she asked him, 'why did you do this?' 'What are a few white lies entre amants,' shrugged Jean-Paul and pushed his way past her. 'Get out!' Maria screamed. 'Les femmes, oh les femmes!' he sighed. 'Now, Maria, you just pipe down...Easy, easy, we don't want the neighbours to hear - do we? How about a quickie?'

Maria pushed him away. Jean-Paul twisted her round. His arm across her throat, he jerked her elbows back and forced her down on to the carpet. She thrashed with her arms and dug her nails into his wrists. Maria went on struggling, but he was much bigger, heavier and stronger than her. An ice-cold feeling plummeted from her stomach to her bowels. 'I don't mind a bit of resistance,' said Jean-Paul, 'in fact I quite like it.' He forced his tongue into her mouth. She spat in disgust and kicked him, but had little impact. His weight pinned her to the floor. Jean-Paul pulled up her skirt, ripped off her pants and raped her. Maria tried to move her eyes, lift them against the weight of time. My life is falling forwards into an abyss, she thought.

'So, did you enjoy it?' Jean-Paul sniggered. 'It turns many women on...They dream about it...Some begged me to hurt them, to go deeper into them. Quite a few women like a bit of rough and ask for more.' He pulled up his trousers and combed his hair with his fingers. 'It must remain our sweet secret!' he said, his finger mockingly on his thick lips.

Maria felt like screaming and hitting out. She wanted to push him out of the window so that she didn't have to look into his ugly face any more, but he was much stronger than her and she was helpless. She thought about the frailty of sanity and felt herself sinking.

When Jean-Paul had gone, Maria crawled to the kitchen. She

felt hot nausea and rested her cheek against the cool door of the fridge. She closed her eyes.
'Oh dear God, help me!'

After a long time had passed Maria got up. The flower bushes were swaying against the light, their silhouettes trembling eerily. Purple clouds had gathered and were hanging menacingly low. The sulphur-coloured air announced the impending storm. It came in fast, exploding and flashing right over her head.

A week had passed and Peter came back. It was a painful moment for Maria. She put up a hand to his cheek and felt his face. 'Oh, it is you,' she said in quiet recognition. 'Who else?' he replied, good-natured, affable, smiling. His triumphant good humour was hard to bear. Maria felt deeply ashamed; she could not look into his eyes. She felt sick with sorrow at the anguish she could be causing Peter, for the love they had for each other must surely be splendid. What was going to happen now? Tears were brimming on her lower lids. Unaware, Peter was turning his elegant back to her, busily unpacking.

When Peter held her in his arms and they lay face-to-face, Maria's heart gave a lurch. She remembered the first time they had made love. Afterwards he didn't immediately reach for a cigarette, but encircled her afresh with his arms as if to say: 'I love you, let's stay together for ever.' This thought filled Maria with grave exultation. Peter was a kindly man with a great tolerant heart.

He slept like a lead soldier - the sleep of the just. Maria kept tossing and turning. When she woke up, Peter had gone to his office. She got up, stood by the table and fell over. She reached for the phone and told the office that she was unwell. Then she was thought: everything is alright now, Peter is back, I am safe.

It was very quiet in the room. What lay in this silence? Was she still herself? What was self? Maria didn't know and felt weak and empty.
Eventually she dragged on some clothes. I have to struggle against my inclination to see things darker than they are, Maria thought. She looked out of the window. In the neighbour's garden green waves of weeds were foaming in the breeze. A tangerine hammock was hanging between two apple trees. The sun came out with sudden intensity.

I long to go back to the way we were before it happened - back to the innocence, Maria thought. She was thinking about what she would say to Peter when he came home. 'Your partnership with Jean-Paul is turning out to be a disaster,' she would say. 'I think you will have to part with him.' She sighed because how could she back up her reasoning? She could never tell him what had happened - it would destroy them both. Peter must not be aware that dark secrets were lurking round corners.

When Peter eventually came home, he turned on the light, showing up things that were better hidden. Maria wanted him to say something like 'I have wonderful news' and then she would ask him what it was. But this is what Peter said: 'My respect for Jean-Paul increases daily. In my absence he managed to pull off a tremendous business deal.' Maria felt a sickly sorrow like poison going into her. How to warn Peter who knew nothing of Jean-Paul's badness?
Then Peter turned around. 'Are you alright?' he asked. Had he apprehended her distress? 'You are as pale as a ghost,' he said. ' I mean is something the matter?' He looked at her with kind, worried eyes. 'I missed you,' Maria replied. When she put her arms around him, she felt perfect calm, at peace. She wouldn't

have to be afraid any longer, afraid to answer the door. She was possessed by hope, as sweetly and helplessly as a young girl.

Only yesterday Maria thought she would never have unconditional trust again, but suddenly she felt a burst of radiance. For what she had with Peter was something immense and shimmering and sufficient.

Bunny Evans

Bunny is a creative copywriter from Canada, who specializes in window display wording for top major department stores in London and Toronto. She has won awards in New York for Children's animated Christmas windows and has been published in 'Chatelaine' Woman's Magazine.

She has also assisted in public relations on events like 'Caravan,' a nine day Expo encompassing 36 different colourful ethnic nationalities. Recently, Bunny completed a 'Montessori' course for children and would like to pursue writing for children.

DISCOVERY...

Sometimes we discover things about ourselves when we're not even looking. For instance, I have a lot of strong emotion and don't know when it will show itself or how. I have discovered that, if I lose 'someone dear to me,' then the only way I can deal with the force of my feelings ... is by sitting down at the old typewriter keys like some folk sit down to a piano.

Can I give you an example?

I heard from Canada about my auntie dying, (*I can't use that word*) - Perhaps it's better to say, 'gone to another place'. Feeling overcome with grief I stumbled my way to my little typewriter. And wrote this without stopping to punctuate! Would you like to give a listen?

MY AUNT ADA

And how do I remember her?

In the kitchen preparing cheese-dreams and always 'pulling my leg,' but grinning with it - so that I understood 'all was well' - so important to a child.

I had a small black and white check suit case with just enough space for pyjamas and a toothbrush. My mum thought I should have a travel case early on. Think I was only three or more... but what glee... to find it underneath the Christmas tree... So I could be ready to visit my Aunt.
(A discovery as I write, 'my mother knew me well and let me go at an early age.)

I remember Aunt Ada leaving me 'just to be'... and so I sat on the floor in front of an old-fashioned bookshelf delving into Elsie Dinsmore -oh she was such a long-suffering damsel in those Victorian novels, I discovered in that attic.. *How little I knew then about where I would live eventually... (England must have been there in the background, always waiting for me.)*

I remember Aunt Ada being amused as I spilled out adventures, ideas, I felt safe in telling my secrets, acknowledged as a person. And she was my Daddy's sister and there was a likeness.

Once I helped teach my Uncle Four (I was 17) some new dance steps. 'Balmy' was the dance rage in the Beeches area of Toronto and I counted out 1, 2, 3, 4, over and over again as we traced out a box step. Oh, how we three laughed and laughed during that lesson.

I recall my Aunt's garden from a dining room window 'being long with borders of flowers' and neat greenery in the centre.

I remember the veranda - and Panny living next-door - so warm was she - so tall and laughing he... and the son called Alex?

I liked racing down the street. Was it 699? And landing on the mat as I leapt up and rang the bell - it was always exciting to arrive there and be so sure of a welcome.

I seem to remember a giant dining room table and so many gathering around for 'Stitch and Chat' and so much laughter. A famous family story was of my Mother making a whole pot of tea for fifteen ladies with just one tea bag. 'Well,' she said, looking impish, 'it's wartime and don't we all have to conserve?'

I remember Aunt Ada's spirit of fun and adventure... - like in her seventies and swimming with me in Milford Haven, Muskoka, when she was working in Aunt Jessie's hotel. I had come over from Milford Manor and together we swam and sat out together as the sunlight dried us off on a big Northern rock. (From age 6, I remember she had a cutout swimsuit in black, not daring, but very much the fashion of the time.)

I remember babysitting the boys with Aunt Ada at Barbara Crescent (her grandchildren). Me dressed in yellow - trousers and top - and going for a walk down a leafy green path with Doug and Bruce as 'young little men.'

And calling for Doug, my godchild, every Christmas for the Hugh C MacLean Publishing Company's Christmas party in our tiny Nash Metropolitan.

And later, when I lived in Somerset being told by Aunt Ada that, 'she had gone to picnics on the sands at Weston-super-Mare as a child.'

Both times that I lived in England, - once in Somerset and once in London ... hers was the first Christmas card I received.

I had always wanted to be a crafts person. So my aunt started me off knitting with pink string. I was to make a dishcloth but she kindly said when finished - 'Shall we give it a little Fairy Liquid dear? My little fingers taking so long. How could pink turn so grey!'
But that dishcloth was my gift to her - and whatever I gave was good enough.
(Another discovery -)
I was started off royally by a Royal Aunt - I loved my aunt Ada.

HIS NAME WAS REG

His name was REG.
MY FIRST FRIEND IN LONDON TOWN.

He came out of the Porter's House and introduced himself -
'YES, IT'S THE SAME AS THE STREET...   REG
CARNABY ...'
'WELCOME TO LONDON!!!'

And so he twinkled away, with a mischievous grin, rocking
back and forth on his heels, just outside Wynnstay Gardens,
near Allen Street in Kensington W8.

One day seeing my plight, *(I was often the maiden in distress)*
Reg helped me to hang some very exotic curtains delivered
from Canada. These were in the palest turquoise blue with the
lights of mauve shading through. Named Fantasia, as they had
a wonderland mood, they were to go in my 'Somerset' room at
No. 34.

Perhaps the red William Morris paper, the gold satin cushions,
the grey velvet sofa bed from Biba's were a little Hollywood for
No. 34 but NOT for Reg.

Reg listened to my stories of living in Somerset and my life in
Canada and decided to introduce Tony and I to Rene, his wife.

And so began a four-way friendship, and then a six-way
friendship with two furry little friends... Tutley, our male cat,
hiding under a blanket and playing games with Rene... and
Esmarelda snuggling up to Reg when he was kitten-sitting.

These two favoured pussycats longed for Christmas (when we were away) ... they were served roast turkey when the Carnaby's came to call. *(oh, I wish had their generosity of spirit).*

Once, the proper Mrs. Craster, living one floor below, complained about Mr. Nesbitt's loud music and rang Reg to be the mediator and to please request 'turn down the volume' ... it was at 10 a.m. on a Saturday morning.

We were informed that 'the music is carrying all the way downstairs, please turn it down. 'But,' and with a smile... 'Mrs. Craster does like Mr. Nesbitt's taste in operatic music.' Reg knew about diplomacy.

And will we ever forget the Sailor's Hornpipe Dance at a party. The floor was cleared. The furniture moved back. And Mr. Carnaby showed us to how to properly do this dance!

When we got engaged it was to Rene that I ran. I was just so excited and thrilled that I literally raced down to her flat, (which by the way was usually filled with little signs from all the tenants reading 'please feed our fish' etc).
You see I instinctively knew where the warmth and character resided.
With the Carnaby's.

When my Mother, Mabiette, or Mabel as she was also called, came to stay, Reg and Rene invited her on a rather exclusive pub-crawl in Kensington. I don't think she ever forgot it! Down Allen Street, along to Abingdon Road and over to the Queen Victoria, finally down Earl's Court Road to a delicious fish and chip supper. Mabel talked about that treat from the Carnaby's for years.

I don't suppose any two helped us more. Around them, it always felt good to be open and human. Oh, there were always jokes, about the boiler room having to be checked by Reg when he wanted a quiet hour. And Ms. Bun stretched out with Ernie the tall electrician, figuring out an antiquated electrical system and learning about 3-socket plugs. (She even carried this in her pocket for a whole week much to Reg's amusement). 'Does John Lewis stock these?'

We followed the Carnaby Family to their new flat and school in Greenwich - because they were now caretakers to the teachers and the children in this lovely part of London.
We always took a turkey and shared a meal at Christmas.

If Reg were here, he would have such a giggle over my starting back to school in 1995, to study MONTESSORI. It's the Italian method of teaching 2 to 7 year olds at the St. Nicholas Teaching Institute in Knightsbridge. It very progressive and great fun.

I won't worry over Reg. He's now caretaking in heaven. Esmarelda (our cat) is up there and will cuddle up to him and Mabel (my Mother) will wise-crack about fish and chips and all three will be in each other's good company.

He was and is our friend. And that fellow Gemini spirit never far away.

DISCOVERY: Making the connection is the most important thing in life. See how my Mother turns up again in this story, always adding in the element of fun. And how the drama is always right there in front of us, in our everyday lives. It's up to us to step into the play. And enjoy!

Lucy Edwardes

Lucy has been writing for the past year and a half, she took a year out, temping and attempting to get published commercially. This is her first effort. She is now organising the recruitment and training for an image consultancy as well as continuing a creative writing course with Kensington and Chelsea College. She has lived in Fulham for approximately three and a half years.

BETRAYAL OR DISCOVERY?

'It would be really good for you to meet Charlie sometime, I'll ring next week', said Harriet's voice on the answer phone. Sarah breathes deeply and exhales a slow waiting breath. At last communication with the other side, it had taken this long! Would she ever be able to make up the lost ground? In her guts she feared not, (too many mistakes previously for that) but she missed shared laughter and revelry that seemed to be evading her life these days.

Sarah observed the second hand ticking on ominously as the week vanished into the past. Hope for her is like a netted butterfly fluttering at the speed of sound, constantly expecting the phone to ring. As for Harriet, events in her life have moved on and she does not get round to ringing next week.

Sarah's butterfly slows down inside her chest to a slow rhythmic beat, just concentrating on being alive - a monumental effort. Sleep eludes at her night so she uses it as a shield during daylight hours to blot out her misery. She can't continue like this, it's consuming her, taking up all her thoughts and actions. She decides to take what she thinks is a constructive step and make that call again, using a positive, chirpy sounding voice. Harriet repeats, 'I'll ring sometime when Julian gets back from his business trip.' Sarah would love to go around and help out with the baby. The butterfly stops drooping; begins to beat its wings again. A little wisdom is there now, the beat more steady and persistent. As time goes on it slows, but does not stop completely.

Flipping through the paper one morning a particular line in 'Alex' (the cartoon strip in the Daily Telegraph) caught her eye.

The last caption has the closing line, 'If you want to show how little you value someone, you just don't return their calls'. Man, that bought it home to her. What was she doing wasting her time? The cartoon summed it up in one. She cut it out of the paper and attached it to the fridge. Her own private reminder of her foolishness; people would enjoy the joke and she'd appreciate the warning.

Life continued normally, getting up, eating, drinking, and doing what she had to do. Her other half Nick said he loved her as much as he could. Try as she could to ignore it she knew she missed something - LAUGHTER - the sort that could lead to a bellyache and sore ribs. She recognises it in other people, from their gestures, meaningful eye-meets, and the jokes that would be exploded over later; once out of eye and earshot.

When Nick answered the telephone, loud laughter reverberated round the house lightening the atmosphere. The butterfly began to flutter lightly in anticipation of some shared laughter. The phone clunks down - end of conversation - silence creeps back out of the floorboards again.

She wanders downstairs and smiles thinking to herself 'PMA equals Positive, Mental, Attitude, walk in look nonchalant and ask off hand what they laughed about (trying not to reek of desperation).

'Anyone interesting?' she asked with a raised eyebrow. 'Yeah, Dan', he nodded.
'On form?' she quizzed, 'Yeah as ever,' he replied not looking up from the TV guide. 'About anything in particular?' she carried on, ignoring his rudeness and cursing her own insecurity.

'He wondered if I would like to play pool sometime and have a few beers, a bit of a lads session.' He told her.

'Sounds good to me, make the most of it' she replied. He looked pleased, relief shone in his eyes.

Sitting there she thought: 'why am I putting up with all this crap? Why not just go and to hell with the lot of them' That could be classed as running away and not solve anything. Too late, she had thought 'the thought', which wedged itself in her sub consciousness and refused to budge.

While she was at work on Friday her tenants called to say they were moving out and would replace the glasses they had broken. These people were good friends she would be sad to see them go. Time for the next stage of married life: to buy out Nick's cousins share of the house. Her mouth went dry and furry at the thought but she carried on.

At twenty to six she stepped off the tube and walked down to St Maur Roads towards Fulham Road. As she turned the corner she breathed in the aroma of fresh flowers. A moments respite for her nose from sweaty bodies and petrol fumes!

Automatically she stopped at the Zebra crossing waiting for the vehicle to slow down - a familiar colour dark grey, followed by the number plate and the VW badge. Inside a young couple and a baby seat, clothes hanging from the hook at the back. She blinked, recognised them straight away, not a flicker of an eyelid from the passengers, just blank fish eyes watched as she walked by. She caught a comment with her eye, apparently demeaning in its delivery by the receptive smirk on the man's face. The car drive off; moment over.

Her butterfly beat an angry rhythm realising that was it, but still she felt hurt, humiliated. Why say ring her and then not - people are so strange. Though who was she to judge? After all one person's hurt is another person's wisdom.

She was glad to put the key in the front door. Clattered her bag down on the floorboards and switched the answer phone off. Nick's voice comes out of nowhere 'I'm having a drink with the finance people after work, I'll see you later'
'Thank God' she shouted back at the answer phone.

She flopped on the sofa and felt everything slowly seep out of her. 'What a bitch of a day,' she thought. She was looking forward to a mindless evening of watching TV. As for the other thing she threw it in her mind's dustbin where hopefully it would stay.

An episode of Friends and Jo Brand made her laugh out loud and mirth poured back into her.

Sarah picked out Rats by Sass Jordan, pressed play and listened to it with the lights out. She remembered taking it for a test drive in HMV. Sarah had shut her eyes and let it wash over her. It slammed hard on the shore of her brain pounding at her temper and temporarily drowned the doubts from her skull. Her rock and roll odyssey was interrupted by a loud doorbell ring.

She turned on the outdoor light before answering and peered through the spy hole, Nick looked at her, his face white and moonlike.
She opened in haste, 'What happened? You look terrible.'
'I've been mugged, my jacket was slung over my shoulder then two young lads appeared out of nowhere on Varna Road and snatched it from my fingers. I gave chase for about fifty yards and gave up. They were too fast for me'.

He followed her into the sitting room where she lit him a cigarette, he accepted it and crashed back into the chair. She sat and carefully contemplated the ceiling before opening her mouth. 'Okay?' she asked trying to sound casual.

He looked up, nodded, 'Yeah, I'll be fine.' His head flopped sideways and he exhaled quietly. Sarah's mind rushed through three possible courses of action. Ring the police. Cancel the credit cards. See if they had abandoned the jacket. At least if they found that, it would save the purchase of a new suit. 'Are you going to ring he police and credit card people?' she asked positively in his direction.
He nodded and plodded over to the phone to make the necessary calls. They sat and waited in silence for the police to come. Instinctive affection made her want to reach out to him but intuition held her back. His personal space had been violated enough for one night, the last think he needed was some puppy love. That's how he would think of it anyway.

Two policemen showed up one thin and thick, the other brawn and brains. 'Thin and thick' was considerate and wiped his boots on the doormat, she appreciated the gesture. Brawn and brains became efficient and took notes, made sympathetic noises and asked the right questions. Had Nick cancelled his credit cards? He went on to say that he doubted if they would recover the wallet, but they might find the jacket, if they were lucky, this was a very common crime in the area etc etc. With that thin and thick beamed at Sarah, fat and clever nodded at them both and then they stomped off in to the night.

Sarah and Nick both agreed that the thin policemen were the least intelligent of the two. He had just repeated everything the other one had said. 'Perhaps he was in training,' Sarah suggested wanting to be fair. 'I doubt it, ' said Nick. They grinned at each other in silent conspiracy. She sat and waited thinking they should go and look for the jacket. Nick pushed his glasses back on his nose and said to her 'Shall we go and look for my jacket, then at least I won't have to replace my suit.'

They both jumped a foot in the air as the telephone interrupted them. Nick grabbed it frowning. Sarah watched him nodding slowly becoming more confident as the conversation went on. He put the phone down and said, 'Someone's found my wallet on the ground. There's no cash in it, but all the cards are there. I'm going to collect it and search fro my jacket as well.'

She felt relief for him. Combining stretching with a standing up motion, she asked him if he would like some company out there in the big bad world. He looked at her and nodded, alcohol glazing his eyes. It was cold outside and Sarah huddled up to him, he stiffened, and she withdrew. For the moment, a neat line had been drawn down the middle of them and neither strayed over it. While he went to collect his cards, she scoured the rubbish bins and pavement for his jacket but there was no sign of it. If only. From the shadows she watched him walk crookedly down the stairs and felt tenderness for him.
'Hi, get them ok?' she said smiling at him.
'Yeah - good news, isn't it,' said Nick looking pleased. 'It's a bummer about the jacket thought, it'll cost me a fortune to replace it.'
'Shame it's not just a dry-cleaning bill you have to fork out for,' Sarah said. 'Did you enjoy your drink?'
'I did,' Nick responded, 'and hopefully I'll get lots of commission out of them in the future.' With that comment they reached the front door and Sarah unlocked it. 'Do you want a glass of water?' Nick asked.
'No thanks,' she replied.

She wandered into the sitting room, where Nick joined her. He lit a fag, and she looked at him lovingly and full of concern. All her worry came out from a safe distance where hopefully he would not feel smothered. He immediately shot her his most filthy look, 'Stop staring can't you? Haven't you seen anyone who's been mugged before?'

Sarah felt her brain detach itself from her body. It floated just above her head where it hovered looking down at the scene unfolding before it. The brain watched the mouth open and out came the words, 'I care, that's all.' Her mouth turned down at the corners.
'You really don't know how to handle yourself, do you baby?' Nick responded looking at her in a detached manner.

'I handle myself as me and I can't do it any differently from that,' she replied. The brain instructed her body to stand up. It did so. The body bent over picked up its handbag and the brain instructed it to walk out the front door. 'That was easy wasn't it?' said her brain to her body as the front door slammed behind them. Sarah felt whole with herself once more. She drove over to her flat and spent the night on the floor. She slept like a baby and woke feeling much refreshed. From that moment without Nick by her side the world seemed a clearer place. She appreciated the space last night's sudden action had brought her. She felt a guilty twinge about Nick, but she was more worried about getting to work on time, Nick could wait till later.

Sarah arrived at work to the curious stares of her colleagues all dying to hear something out of the ordinary. She told them nothing apart from that she had had a bad night; an argument. She got her work done a lot more quickly that morning as there were no candidates to distract her, and there was no background noise in her brain.

Nick rang her at lunchtime and she was calm, offhand with him, no hysteria. There was no need for it; actions speak louder than words. 'Well, when are you coming home then?' Nick asked straight away. 'When I'm ready' she told him.

'I'm sorry about last night,' he said. 'Let's discuss it later, she replied aware that Doreen was taking longer than needed to make her coffee. The conversation moved on from there to the everyday.

Nick told her with a groan about his boss being anal as usual. Sarah told him about Harriet on the Pedestrian Crossing.

'Oh Sarah, it's me isn't it?' he sighed.

'You know that Harriet says, she will ring me 'sometime next week' and never gets round to it. I am now convinced it's a lost cause and she doesn't care anymore. Problem is I miss the laughs we used to have. They were these huge bellyaches that I seem to have lost the knack for nowadays and I need some practise otherwise I'll wither up.' The telephone sighed into her ear, 'Perhaps we could try' a voice suggested tentatively. She smiled down the telephone, 'I'd like that,' she said and hung up very softly.

Caroline Walker

Caroline has been a member of Women's Ink since joining the morning writing group (then Wednesday Women) in January 1997. She has been an active member ever since, and is currently Chair of the group. She writes for pleasure, although not yet for publication. Her work also involves writing - she is an editor and has recently published a student guide to careers in the law.

THIRTY-TWO

Laura was thirty then. Then, when it happened. She was successful, on target. Writing for the nationals, getting a reputation, in demand. She had a little flat in Notting Hill. She had bought it just before Notting Hill got seriously trendy. After several years of fluctuations she had her weight just where she wanted it, curves kept firmly in place by her personal trainer. She'd found exactly the right shade of auburn for her hair, had her colours tested at 'Colour-Me-Beautiful'. Knew what suited her.

Laura was thirty then. Thirty when she lost it. 'Lost' implies accident, it implies lack of control, implies carelessness. All of these were involved. Yes, certainly they were involved.
She was thirty when it happened. Thirty and she had her friends, too many to keep up with, spread all over the world now, successful like her. Useful contacts. She had lovers, no one fixed, nothing permanent. She had long ago rejected the loss of independence that word 'relationship' encompassed. Had long ago settled on living her own life, doing her own thing. Concentrating on career. Her family she saw at Christmas. They looked out for her name in their daily newspapers. Her mother bragged about it. 'Our daughter' she'd say. 'Front page of the Guardian. Shame it's not The Times but she always had her left-wing views.'

Laura was thirty. Thirty when she curled her lip at friends with their eternal needs, their biological clocks ticking towards desperation. Their dating agencies and dinner parties and longing looks into Baby GAP window.

Thirty. And sometimes, just sometimes, the champagne would

flow and that unknown man would seem subtly more attractive. Another glass and another. And what was independence for? If not for this, for thoughtless touches and excited encounters, for not having to get used to him.

She was thirty when her breasts began to swell. When her rounded belly and clothes too tight and too many weeks gone by all began to add up. All posed questions. Leading to one answer. She was thirty when she made the appointment, thirty when she rearranged her diary, cancelled her interviews, skipped that book launch, penned neat little red asterisks against the first and second of the month. When she phoned her friends and joked that she was off to Paris for a couple of days with a new man. They hadn't met him. They wouldn't meet him. He was married. She was thirty when she checked into the clinic in her smart suit. Sat in the waiting room, looked at the others, at all the others, at their sad disorganised lives. Looked at their sad careless lives. Looked at the mess they'd made of their lives. The wasted lives. She was thirty then.

She's thirty-two now. And as she sits in for another night playing with her hair she stares into space. And thinks he would have been a year old now. And thinks he would have been a year old. And thinks of a little romper suit. In the window of Baby GAP.

THE FLIGHT OF ICARUS

Oh the heights, the soaring, dancing, gasp of air, touch the sun ecstatic heights.

When the wise master craftsman Daedalus made the wings of feather and of wax for his only son Icarus he gave him a solemn and stern warning. 'Icarus my son. These wings I have made for you are not the wings of birds. They are wings made of man and not of God. When you fasten the straps of leather onto your shoulders, and feel the weight of your plumage, you will catch the fancy of the breeze and she will dance with you. But beware. The tempting winds will caress you. Will carry you up into the path of the Sun. And the sun is a god and not to be flirted with. Should you become bedazzled and bewitched by his beauty - should your euphoria carry you away to heights never dreamt of by man, you will fall. Man cannot lift himself too high from his body of clay. Too high and too brilliant your dance and the sun will melt your feathers away from you and you will fall. And you must fall. But beware the fear of the sun. For should you keep too low, skulk beneath the siren winds and hover where the sun cannot touch you, your wings will be drenched by the spray of the wine dark sea. Your wings of feather and of air will become leaden with water, and you will fall. And you must fall. For man should not hide away from the sunlight and the glory, should not keep to the darkness and the depths. For this too is bad. You are a man, my son, not a god. Yet nor either a lowly creature. So do not seek to play with the gods and soar beyond man's reach. But do not deny all knowledge of the gods and of your own capacity. Both ways mean disaster. Think on my words, oh Icarus, and I wish you God speed.

And the young and golden boy took up the massy wings of

leather and of wax and of feathers crafted by the good Daedalus. And as he flexed his taut young muscles and felt the breeze softly caressing his skin he felt a yearning inside him. He felt a longing for the heights, the utmost heights, the blue vault of the sky. And he let the wind play with him and toss him at her will. And he closed his eyes and exulted. His father's words rang in his head. But the midday heat soon melted them away. 'The Sun is a benificent god. He will not harm me, he could not. Look how he shines for me. Feel how he loves to caress my skin. Hear how he calls me near.' And higher and higher he flew, arching and swooping and glorying in himself, towards the hypnotic disc of the sun.

Down, down below, on his prison island far below, stood Daedalus. And he wrung his hands and wept but could do nothing. For in Icarus' position wouldn't he have done the same? Would he not have touched the sun? Would he not have sacrificed all for this one heady chance? And, even as he watched, the wax dripped inexorably down the powerful arms of his only-born son. And a perfect grey downy feather floated past his window, to be caught by the grey spray from the waiting ocean below.
And still his son soared ever higher.

Oh the heights, the soaring, dancing, gasp of air, touch the sun ecstatic heights.

Sade Adeniran

Sade is an IT Consultant and has been writing part-time since she graduated from university. Her play 'Memories of a Distant Past' was commissioned by Radio 4 for the 1995 Young Writers Festival. The following extract is from her upcoming novel 'Just Imagine This'

JUST IMAGINE THIS

'Whatever the eyes of
a dead man see
in the burial yard
is caused by death'
Yoruba Proverb

1st January 1991

Dear diary,
When I was a child I spoke like a child and acted like a child. Now that I am grown I put my childish ways behind me and view the world with a weary cynicism that has become hard to shake. How I miss the wonders of an innocence lost, yet I was never innocent. I miss the lightheartedness of a happy childhood spent knowing that I was loved by those who made me, yet a child I never was. I grew up too soon, too fast, taunted with the knowledge of what I never had but lost.

They say the struggles of man begin at birth, my struggles really began in Idogun. I prevailed because to resign oneself to one's fate is to be crippled fast. I won, not because I had courage, neither was I strong. I simply wanted what I didn't have. So I begin again, another struggle and as Time turns the page, my life inevitably goes on. This is what was, it has shaped my present, by learning from my mistakes and my arrogance I'll let it shape my future. Who knows I might even get to live happily ever after like a princess in a fairytale.

18th January 1979

Dear diary,
I am not a happy person, my plan did not work. I thought I

would be expelled for sure but when I went to the Principal to tell him it was me, he put me on labour for 3 days. Which means that I have to work on the school farm for 3 whole days, it's just not fair.

19th January 1979

Dear diary,

I don't have to work the 3 days anymore 'cos Remi came to my rescue, so did my ex-arch enemy Dorcas. They both went to the Principal on my behalf and told him that it was Jumoke who started the witch-hunt, and that she said she'd beat me up if I didn't say it was me. So Jumoke got 10 days' labour, 6 for the original 3 and 4 for threatening to beat me up. She doesn't like me very much at the moment, but it's not my fault 'cos if she wasn't such a coward in the first place she wouldn't have 10 labour days.

31st January 1979

Dear diary,

I got a letter from Adebola today, for the first time my name was called out in assembly when it came to giving out letters.
Ivy Secondary School
P.M.B 13002
Ado Ekiti
Ondo State

16th January 1979

Dear Sis,

Happy new year, did you make any new year resolutions? I couldn't think of anything I needed to change apart from leaving this place and it's not in my power to change that. How are you anyway? I hope this letter reaches you in good health. Things have gone from bad to worse with Uncle J, he works me like a servant instead of treating me like his nephew. Lola we'll have to do something about our situation, maybe running away would be the better option 'cos quite frankly I can't take much more of this. I think we should've taken off when we had the chance in London, it will be harder here but I'll get a job and take care of you since our father isn't really up to the job, we'll just have to wait till I'm a bit older.

All I seem to do is clean, clean and clean. If anything needs doing, whose name is it that gets called? ADEBOLA. Adebola do this, Adebola do that, go here go there. According to Uncle J, it's training for when I get married. If my wife can't clean then I can shame her into it by doing it myself. When I get married I intend to hire a maid to do all the cleaning.

I've been ill, but I'm getting better. Uncle J says it's as a result of the blast in the face that I got during the memorial. I thought I was going to go blind, but my eyes are okay and the skin is healing gradually. Since I haven't been to school since term started I have a lot to catch up on when I do go back. The good news which I should have told you first is that I got a letter from daddy and I'll be able to board next year. I'll only see Uncle J during the Christmas and Easter hols. the long ones we'll spend together with daddy in Lagos.

So I'll be seeing you in July or is it August? Anyway when we see each other we can try softening daddy up and see if he'll change his mind. We might get lucky, but don't get your hopes up, I don't think he wants 2 kids cramping his style. Remember that I love you even if you are a pain, sometimes I miss you (when I don't remember you as the stubborn cow you can sometimes be). Keep your chin up and take care of yourself.

Lots of love and xxxxxxxs
Adebola (Your one and only handsome and suave brother)

He's so silly, sometimes I think they made a mistake with our birth certificates and I'm the eldest. He obviously didn't look up the meaning of suave before he wrote it down, 'cos according to my dictionary it means having smooth and sophisticated manners. Manners is one thing Adebola has none of, he can be such a pig, like burping in my ear after he's finished eating or farting in my face. I'll write back and tell him he won't become prince charming if he carries on the way he does.

I didn't think of a new year's resolution, but the one thing I'm going to try and change is living in Idogun. If every thing goes to plan, I'll either be expelled or I'll fail so miserably that daddy won't have a choice but to let me live with him where he can take a hand in my education, he's the one who's always telling us that it's important to be somebody and the only way to be somebody is with a good education, it will lay one's foundation for life. I think it's more important to him though.

5th February 1979

Dear diary,

Dorcas is sick, well she's mostly sick in the morning, she keeps throwing up and won't eat her food. As her new best friend, she gives it to me especially since she got 30 out of 50 on the last English test. She sat next to me and I let her see some of my answers, luckily she's got a very long neck.

6th February 1979

Dear diary,

Just got back from church, we went to the Methodist in Ugbe and Dorcas fainted. Maybe she's become a witch like Fatima, who isn't coming back to school, or maybe Fatima cast a spell on her before she left. Well that's what Jumoke said to Remi, not that I believe her.

7th February 1979

Dearest diary,

I have the juiciest piece of gossip and I can't wait to tell Remi who's gone to school. I won't be going till 3rd period when I have English. Anyway I was under my bed as usual when Dorcas came back into the dorm, just as I was about to come out and say hello the Principal followed her in. So I just hid, all I could see were their shoes but I think he was kissing her. Yuk yuk yuk, they were really K.I.S.S.I.N.Ging. Then she told him that she doesn't mind becoming his second wife, 'cos now that she's pregnant she doesn't have a choice. But that she wants her own house separate from his other wife. Imagine that, Dorcas pregnant and the Principal is the father, it must have been true about him and Moyin then.

Anyway the Principal said that he loved her, but he has to think of his job and how to feed the 7 children he has already. If he takes her as his 2nd wife then people will know that he got her pregnant and he might lose his job so she'll have to get rid of it and he'll pay for it. I wonder how that happens. Dorcas started to cry and said that if her parents found out that they'd kill her and him, he just said there was nothing he could do and that he had to think of the many instead of the one.
I almost got caught 'cos I nearly sneezed, if that had happened I'm sure he would have done some juju to kill me. He left first then she cried some more then left, I didn't think she'd like it if I'd let her know I heard everything. Imagine Dorcas and the Principal, she probably did it to get good grades, Remi calls it bottom power. She came bottom of the class last term just behind me. She is so dumb, at least I'm not at the bottom of the class 'cos I'm dumb. I just refuse to learn because I have an agenda. It's my new year's resolution. Imagine that Dorcas and the Principal K.I.S.S.I.N.G, I'll only tell Remi 'cos she's my friend.

9th February 1979

Dear diary,
Dorcas's secret is round the whole school, I only told Remi

though, so she must have told other people even though I swore her to secrecy 'cos Dorcas is now my friend. Gbenga is very upset (her boyfriend) and he smashed the windows of the Principal's car, I thought he was going to have a fight with the principal but Mr Abraham took him away to calm him down.

10th February 1979

Dear diary,

Gbenga, (Dorcas's now ex-boyfriend) has been expelled from school. The Principal called him out on assembly this morning and said that due to his act of vandalism and hooliganism he was no longer welcome. Gbenga started to call him horrible names and said that he's nothing but a womaniser who keeps on giving his students babies and that he hasn't heard the last of it. The Principal then tried to deny everything, he said that these were false rumours and he has never given a student a baby (something along those lines anyway) I wish I could have come out and told what I heard but Dorcas is my friend and she's already starting to suspect I started it. She doesn't know for sure though.

11th February 1979

Dear diary,

I got called into the Principal's office today. He wanted to know if it was me who started the rumour but I denied it. Then he wanted to know where I was yesterday morning so I said I was in class, he pulled out the register and showed me I was marked absent. I just told him that I was late and the register had been marked before I got to class. I forgot all about my new year's resolution, well maybe he wouldn't have expelled me for repeating what is true, but I know I'd probably get some lashes from his horse whip that he uses on special students. He hasn't used it on me yet, he probably knows that daddy is an ex-boxer who might come and beat him up if he hurts me.

13th February 1979

Dear diary,

Dorcas went home yesterday, (I think she went home), Aase picked her up very early in the morning on his way to Lagos. I gave him a letter to give to daddy, there wasn't really anything much to say other than that I'm having a miserable time and that I miss him and that I want to go back to London and I'd also like my bike.

The cooks have refused to cook and the food stores are locked so we have to go to the school farm and dig up some yams. We'll have to eat it with palm oil and salt which is the only thing not locked up in the store. Remi and Jumoke have decided to go home and come back in the evening. I wish I had somewhere to go other than the school farm.

14th February 1979

Dear diary,

The cooks are still not cooking so the Prefects had to choose some of the big girls to cook for the whole school and it tasted better than what those cooks make. I think they should let them continue to cook for the school. We had rice and beans on a Monday, we normally have cold nasty eba and watery okra. But I'd take watery okra over starving any day. Almost all the girls got a Valentine's card today, apart from Remi and me. Then again the boys are only after the girls with breasts, I hope I never get any.

17th February 1979

Dearest diary,

All this trouble is my fault, I should have kept my big mouth shut. Gbenga's mother came to school today very upset. She tied her head-scarf around her waist, her hair was all messy and needed to be plaited again. Anyway she turned up during assembly and started crying and begging the Principal to let Gbenga come back to school, since he's the first born son he needs to get a good job so that he can take care of his brothers since their farm isn't doing too well. The price of coca has fallen and they didn't have a very good harvest last year so things are rough and will get worse too. He needs to get a good education so he won't have to work on the farm. The Principal just said there was nothing he could do, and that he has to set an example and remove the bad apple from the cart.

I felt so bad, if I hadn't told Remi then no one but me would've known and Gbenga would still be in school and his mother wouldn't be in tears. I wonder if I had a mother whether she'd cry for me if I ever got expelled from school. Would she get down on her knees like Mama Gbenga and beg the Principal to show mercy. Just imagine that.

18th February 1979

Dear diary,

Today was the day where bottles flew and stones whistled over heads or knocked some heads. There was a riot between our school and Ireakari Grammar School which is in the next village. It was our turn to host the unfriendly football match, last time it was in Idoani and we won 2-0. We beat them on there own ground and victory was sweet, not that I saw the match. I didn't feel like walking the 8 miles it would have taken to get there, so most of the girls stayed behind and the boys went off and came back singing sweet songs of victory.

In the last game we played we had Gbenga who is the best footballer in the whole school, his nickname is Pele and as soon as he gets the ball a roar goes up. Anyway, since he'd been expelled I overheard Mr Abrahams say that winning would be like digging a well with a needle. Not much hope there in the rest of the team. Anyway the game starts and before you know it we were 3 down and didn't look like scoring a goal, that was until Mr Bamijoko decided to put Gbenga on even though he was expelled and no longer a student. By half time we were level and it wasn't even Gbenga who scored the goals. Then Alaba and her big mouth (Alaba is related somehow) goes and tells her brother who happens to go to Ireakari that Gbenga is no longer a student. Of course he had to go and tell his sports teacher, as you can imagine tempers rose and fists flew, then stones then bottles. They broke most of the classroom windows, but we chased them back to their school (not all the way). I don't think the Principal will be too pleased when he finds out what's happened to his school, they even trampled all over the flowerbeds. Jumoke got hit by a stone and I think it was Remi who threw it, but I'm not saying anything. I even saw Titi and Veronica fighting, I think it must have been over Dipo. He likes them both but he liked Titi first but now he likes Veronica who is prettier, so now they hate each other and they used to be best friends. I'd never fight with my best friend over a man, we should be able to share him, like I had to share my toys with Adebola when we were younger. He still has my Orinoco teddy. I still haven't received a reply to my last letter, I hope he's better now and Uncle Joseph isn't being horrible to him.

22nd February 1979

Dear diary,
You'll never guess what happened today. The Oba who never leaves his palace unless a sacrifice is made (it's not like a proper palace like in the fairy stories) came to school with Mama Gbenga today. It was 3rd period and I had English (the only reason I was in school at that time). Two men held a big umbrella over him, it wasn't a rain umbrella. He was being carried on a chair by another two men and the last man was

carrying a large feather fan which he was using to fan the Oba. It was the first time I saw him, he didn't turn up for the memorial 'cos he was ill, according to Bimpe he almost died. Well anyway, they stood outside our classroom which is next to the Principal's office and Mrs Jacobs the Secretary had to bring the Principal out 'cos it is a taboo for the Oba to enter a house without there being a sacrifice to the Gods and his Ifa consulted to make sure it is safe to enter. When the Principal came out he had to prostrate in front of the Oba, he was wearing his favourite white suit. The Oba wanted to know why the Principal wouldn't let Gbenga back in school and that he is a young man with his future ahead of him and it wasn't for the Principal to snuff out his bright light. The Principal wasn't allowed to get up, the man with the fan put his foot on the Principal's back and still managed to fan the Oba. The Principal must have said something 'cos then the man with the fan hit him on the head and we thought he was going to give him lashings of the cane. Mr Abraham tried to continue the lesson but we were too busy gawking at what was happening to the Principal. I wonder if he'll take it out on Bimpe. When he was allowed to get up there was a big footprint on his back and his front was dirty. I felt really sorry for him, only for a little while though 'cos he gave me the evil eye and I had to try and pretend that I didn't see what happened although that was sort of difficult considering that all the students were looking through the broken windows. I overheard Mr Abraham say that it is not good for a chicken to challenge the lion who is the king of the jungle, 'cos it stands no chance of winning. I suppose the Principal is the chicken and the lion is the Oba who has given an almighty roar and frightened poor Principal into submission. I guess from the look of things Gbenga will be coming back to school, the Principal dare not go against the Oba's wishes. Not if he wants to live in this village.

23rd February 1979

Dear diary,

Gbenga is in school again, just as I thought he would be and he has been transferred to my class which is nearer to the Principal's office. We're the first ones who get into trouble for making too much noise, by the time he has finished with our class the bush wire has gone through to the other classes that he's on the move. I've only been caught once, but since I've swapped my desk for a window one I keep one eye on his office door and the other on whatever fun is going on. If someone I don't like is making a lot of noise I don't alert them when he sneaks out with his cane in hand. Because of this I've noticed that most of them are nice to me especially Seyi who buys me lunch every so often. He even gave me his maths set, pity I can't stand maths.

1st March 1979

Dear diary,

Dorcas is back and she is no longer pregnant but she still looks sick. She arrived this morning with her parents and one of her brothers who is very important. I was hiding under my bed when they arrived and I dared not come out. If I had Dorcas would've known for sure it was me who spilled the beans. They dropped off her stuff in the dorm and then went to school. I wondered if the Principal would have to prostrate again because Dorcas told me once that her dad is an Oba too, which I don't believe. If it were true he'd have two people carrying him and one fanning him like the Oba of Idogun. The only thing that made him look like an Oba was the beads he was wearing round his neck, he was fat and he also carried a horse's tail and a carved stick. I followed them but didn't find out what happened, maybe I'll worm it out of Dorcas. I wonder what happened to the baby.

3rd March 1979

Dear diary,

Dorcas is not talking to me, I think she knows it was me who started the whole mess. I bet the moment she fails the next English test she'll be my best friend again. Nothing much is happening.

8h March 1979

Dear diary,

I've been beaten up by Akin, he's been planning his revenge for a long time. I've got a bruise on my head and a cut on my knee, I think I'm going to have to go to the medical centre 'cos it won't stop bleeding. I left class after 4th period Literature with Mr Abraham and he must have followed me. When I was halfway back to the dorm and my hiding place he pounced on me, if he hadn't taken me by surprise he wouldn't have been able to beat me up. I will get my own back on him and make him very sorry he laid a finger on me.

9th March 1979

Dear diary,

My knee hurts so much I can hardly walk, I must have cut it on something sharp when the beast pushed me to the ground. I'm still plotting my revenge and it won't be pleasant. If Adebola was here I'd get him to beat him up. Why do people always pick on me, I haven't done anything to them, it seems that my very existence annoys them. All I have to do sometimes is open my mouth and someone starts to make fun of me, it's just not fair. It seems I'll have to work harder at failing the end of the year exams. Not that it would be very difficult, since the only lessons I've been for are English and Literature.

His Evilness wouldn't let me go to the medical centre, not that I could have walked there, I even have a better excuse to stay in the dorms for the next week. If any of the Prefects find me after bed check I'll just tell them I can't walk to class. I've had to tear off the edge of the wrapper Mama gave me to bind the wound so that flies won't get in and lay their eggs. Baba Ojo showed me what leaves to put on a wound to make it heal, so I guess I'll go to the medical centre when I can walk properly. At least it's Saturday tomorrow and I won't be going to the farm with everyone else. I wonder how long this agony will last 'cos I don't think I can take much more. I wish Adebola was here with me, things aren't so bad when he's around. I guess I'll just have to wait till the long holidays to see him.

14th March 1979

Dear diary,
I think my leg is getting worse and not better, it's all swollen and yellow stuff mixed with blood is coming out when I squeeze it to try and make the swelling go down. I had to go to school today because the Principal did the bed checks and when he saw me lying there he made me get up and put on my uniform. I hate him, he wouldn't leave the room to let me change, then he asked me where my breasts were or didn't they grow them in England. I'm going to tell Daddy and Mama about it. When he saw I really couldn't walk he gave me a lift in his smashed-up car. He's going to bring me back to the dorm and pick me up in the morning, which means I can't even leave class 'cos I can't walk properly.

15th March 1979

Dear diary,
I got a letter from Adebola today, posted almost a month ago, he doesn't sound too happy. It's got two sides so I can't paste it in, but he says that he's still a bit ill and that he hasn't gone back to school 'cos Uncle Joseph says he has to stay at home and get better. But all he does is wash the dishes, wash and iron the

clothes, dust everywhere and make sure there's food on the table when everyone comes home. I suppose he'll have to keep remembering the brighter side of things, soon he'll be in boarding school (I'll be back living with Her Evilness) with no worries at all.

16th March 1979

Dear diary,

Aase just came back from Lagos and I got my first birthday card from daddy in a long time, he wrote me a letter as well. We're moving from the nasty rooms in Orile to a flat in Ikoyi. Adebola and I will have to share a bedroom 'cos there are only two, but that's okay 'cos we've always shared the same room. Maybe this means that we can finally become a family now that we've got a flat. I really didn't want to live in those cramped rooms with the toilet and bathroom in the courtyard shared among the other tenants. I must write to Adebola, he'll be pleased we're finally going to live in Lagos. I'll have to be on my best behaviour all the time 'cos daddy has a short temper and I really don't like stooping down or getting the cane. I'll miss Remi, she's the only friend I have here and without her I don't think I would have been able to bear it much.

I've got some biscuits left, so on Sunday (my birthday) I'll make chocolate drinks for Remi and me and I'll fry the biscuits in butter and celebrate my birthday in style. Maybe I'll make some chocolate as well with what's left of the Ovaltine. What I wouldn't give for chocolate cake, vanilla ice-cream with strawberries, liquorice all-sorts and some curly-wurly's. I'll have that again one day, I promise myself.

17th March 1979

Dear diary,

Uncle Niyi has just turned up at school and I've been told that I have to pack some things and go with him. I wonder if daddy sent him and I'm going to live in Lagos and he's coming to pick me up. This is so exciting, even the Principal was nice to me and he said he'll think happy thoughts for me. I bet he's just glad to get rid of me, Uncle N glared at him when he said that though. Uncle N is pacing up and down the corridor outside the dorm, I wonder what's eating him. I've never seen him like this before, he looks like he's been crying. Well I better finish my packing, not that there's much to pack. I think my leg is getting worse, Uncle N was not pleased at all when he saw that I could barely walk. He was furious with the Principal and told him he should be looking after me properly. It made me feel special. I really should finish packing, I just thought I'd let you know what was going on 'cos I'm so excited.

I refuse to believe it, how can I believe it. Oh dear diary the agony, the absolute agony. Where there were two there is now one, I'm all alone, all alone. Adebola has left me, Uncle Joseph has killed my only brother. Adebola is dead and his body is lying in the other room. When Uncle N pulled up outside Mama's house she rushed out to enfold me to her, I was confused, people were crying as if someone had died. I couldn't think who, Mama was holding me so it couldn't be her. I didn't know what was going on, Uncle N gently led me to Mama's room and there he was, there was my brother lying there with cotton wool stuck up his nose and in his ears. I think I must have screamed, I don't really remember, just that I have no voice, I can't seem to utter a word. I tried to wake him up, I shook him, I took the cotton wool out of his ears so he could hear me calling his name, I tried to make him sit up but he was heavy and cold then they dragged me away. So here I am, now I'm all alone, who will take care of me now, who will stick up for me, who will I run away with when I'm older. What will I do, I don't know what I'll do now that the only person who really loved me is dead. Killed by Uncle Joseph, he probably overworked him, the moment daddy decided to send Adebola to boarding school. I feel such rage, I want to scream till I can scream no more, I want to kill Uncle Joseph. An eye for an eye just like in the Bible. I feel so mad, so mad so mad. No one can explain to me why. Can someone explain to me why? Why did it have to be my brother? What have I done wrong that I lose those I love? First my mother now my brother, can someone please explain why. Where is daddy, why isn't he here? Dear diary the pain is too great, maybe I'll die from it too 'cos I don't think I can bear much more. I see black and I see red and someone is playing the masquerade drums inside my head. Someone please tell me why he had to die. What do I do, what shall I do, my throat is closed and I can't speak, the pain in my knee is nothing to the pain in my chest. I'm all alone, Adebola is dead.